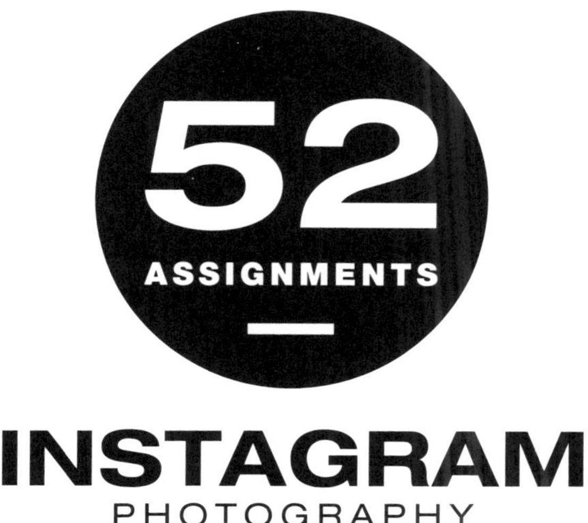

INSTAGRAM
PHOTOGRAPHY

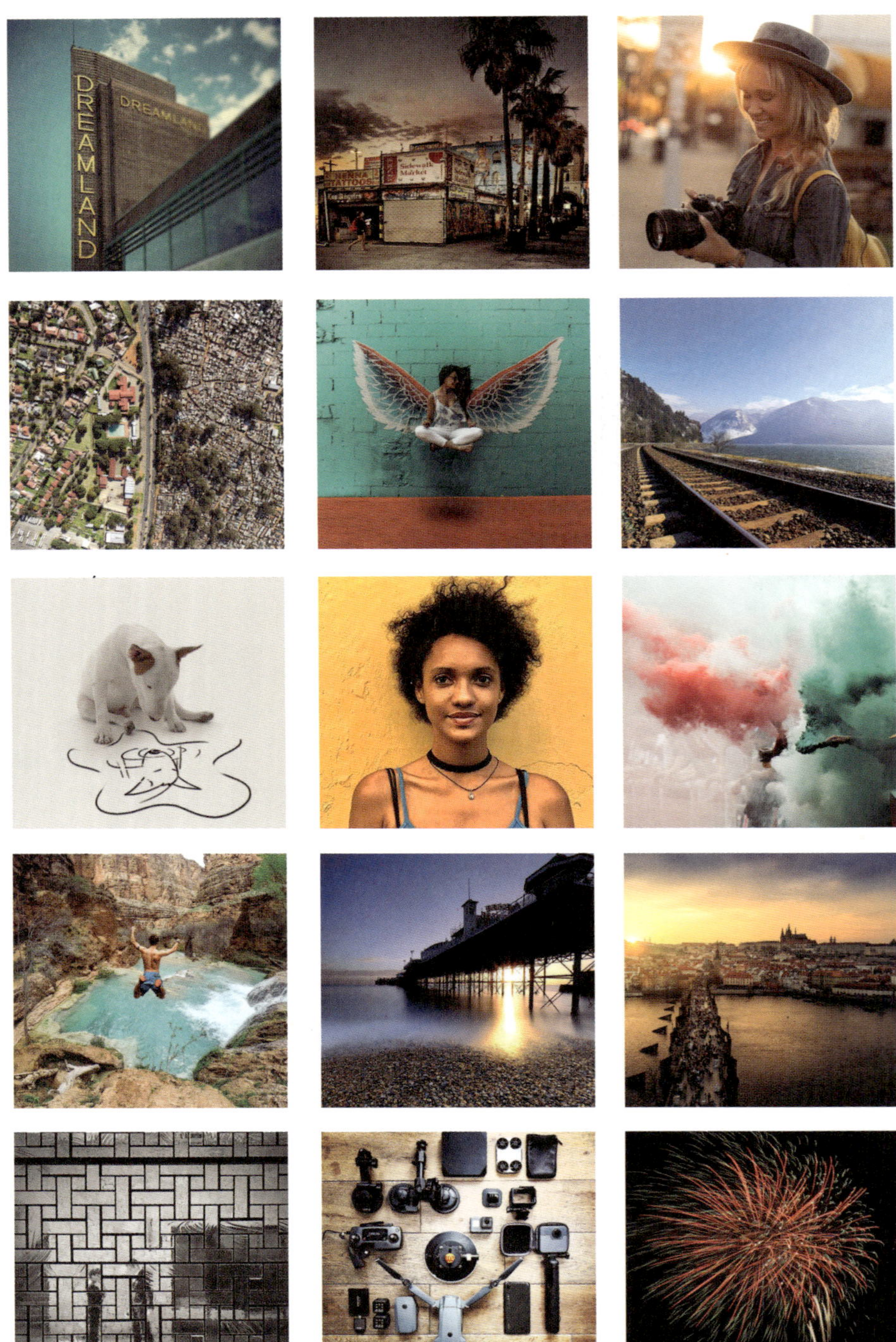

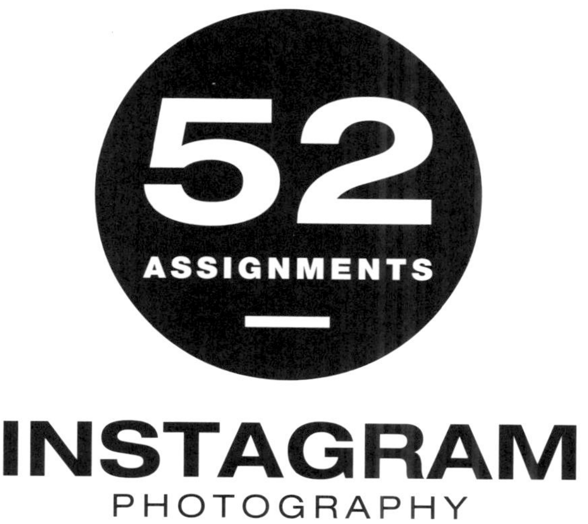

52 ASSIGNMENTS

INSTAGRAM PHOTOGRAPHY

ADAM JUNIPER

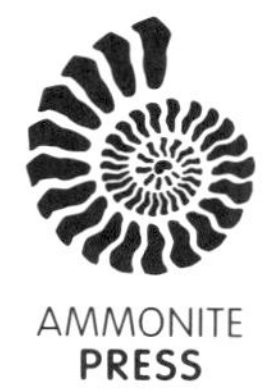

AMMONITE
PRESS

ASSIGNMENTS

Tick off your completed projects

ASSIGNMENT KEY

Each assignment has symbols showing the type of tasks involved.

EDIT

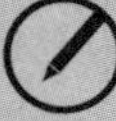 LIGHT AND COLOR

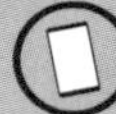 APPS

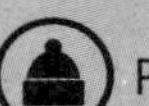 PROPS

HASHTAG

COMPOSITION

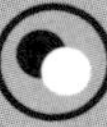 FILTER

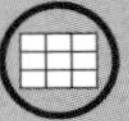  TECHNIQUE

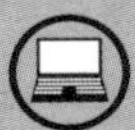 HARDWARE

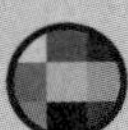

ASSIGNMENT JOURNAL

Use the journal spaces throughout the book to keep a record of your assignments and images.

INTRODUCTION

Assignments are the life-blood of photography, and Instagram provides the veins down which photography now flows. This book will keep your veins pumping.

There are plenty of professional photographers who will bemoan the arrival of Instagram—they'll tell you it has a dumbing down effect and rewards comic snaps of cats over quality photography. By saying that, they're perhaps missing the point. Their minds are tuned to the specific needs of their clients, or imagining the art gallery their work will eventually appear in. Instagram is a new gallery, a different one, and your "clients" are whoever you want them to be.

So, you already know more than some professionals.

That's no cause for complacency, though. Professionals, as a whole, adapt quickly (those who don't won't be professionals any more). But they're just a small part of the very large crowd vying for attention and—because their focus is their client—they're one step behind you. Instagram rewards the spectacular, and you need to stand out in a vast—but level—playing field, where you are just as welcome as anyone else. If you're doing it for yourself, you have another advantage over those whose motives are more commercial. You are free to be creative.

Since you're looking at these pages, it's fair to assume you are hoping to push beyond the courtesy Likes of family and friends and rise into the firmament. Through the 52 photographic assignments in this book, we'll aim to explore and unlock your creative potential so that you can do just that. It might be that we'll help you to find your niche, it might be that you'll find a style you like. We'll try every angle—including shooting with your phone, a camera, accessories, apps, and more—to find ways you can lift your lens above the clouds (literally, in one case).

There are many popular and much-photographed subjects on Instagram (fashion, food, selfies, cats...). Of course you will want to photograph these subjects, and probably already have. Our goal is to show you new ways to do so for greater artistic success, which should lead to more of the Likes you love. My editors and I have chosen a selection of exciting and interesting photographers for you to check out, and we encourage you to follow their accounts to find even more inspiration. Do that, try these assignments—perhaps once a week, perhaps once a day—and your account will take care of itself. Happy shooting!

Adam Juniper
@juniperific

#52assignments #instagram #photography

INSTAGRAM FOR PHOTOGRAPHERS

If you're new to Instagram it will help to get to grips with some of the key concepts and terms that underpin the app before starting the assignments.

FEED

The Feed is the core of Instagram, and is made up of the photographs (and, if you choose, short video clips) that you post. The newest appears at the top, beneath your name and biography. Visitors can scroll down your Feed to see more of your work, tap on the photos, and comment on them. Your images will stay in place on your Feed unless you delete them.

HANDLE

Your "handle" is your unique name within Instagram and starts with an @ sign. Mine is @juniperific. You will sometimes see a blue check mark next to the name of Instagram members, which means the holder is a public figure or celebrity who has asked to have their identity verified by Instagram staff.

POSTING

When you have finished making adjustments to a photograph you can "post" it, which is the action of sending your image to your Feed or story, so the rest of the world can view it. Instagram is designed for you to post images using your smartphone rather than your computer.

FOLLOWERS

While you can always browse the whole of Instagram, it will normally just show you the pictures of those you follow. If you choose to follow someone, you'll be added to their Follower count. Most accounts (70%) have fewer than 1,000 Followers, which include a high percentage of "real people," as opposed to those accounts with very large numbers of Followers, many of which are automated brand accounts, or "bots!"

HASHTAGS (#)

The hashtag symbol (#) is used to flag a piece of metadata by saying "this next word is just a way of explaining what's going on here." This helps out search engines in their effort to catalog the internet. Google is far too smart to need this kind of help, but we humans still use it to indicate what's going on. Instagram makes great use of hashtags, or "tags," to search for related or popular posts.

STORIES

In 2016, Instagram added "stories." These are essentially a different kind of social media—like an app within an app. If your Feed is your permanent record, stories are designed to be transient. They let people know what is happening now. Stories only allow you to post new material (less than 24 hours old) and—except for highlights—that's how long they remain viewable.

IGTV

IGTV, or Instagram TV, is an app that allows longer videos to be uploaded. While the dominant video platform, YouTube, uses the traditional TV format, Instagram stories (including short videos) are viewed in portrait format—the way we hold our phones. Instagram saw a gap for long-form content that didn't immediately disappear, and in 2018 IGTV emerged. More ways of watching videos are appearing all the time.

MESSAGING

Instagram was acquired by Facebook in 2012, who had correctly identified it as a threat. Facebook was already starting to be perceived as being for older users, built as it was when the computers browsing the web ruled—not apps on touchscreen devices such as smartphones. Features like user-to-user messaging have since been added, as well as advertising.

IMAGE-EDITING TOOLS

Filter Instagram allows you to edit photos within the app in a number of pre-defined ways, which it calls filters—these are digital image adjustments, some of which mimic the effects of physical camera filters. The filters vary from time to time, but it's easy to choose by swiping through the previews and tapping on one you like the look of. You can vary its intensity after choosing it.

Edit Instead of applying a filter, you can also choose from a range of photographic edits. These allow you to make adjustments to your picture, such as adding saturation or making a perspective correction, which you can apply to varying degrees in the same way as a filter.

Crop When you first select an image from your phone's camera you can zoom in or out by pinching your fingers on the screen, as well as dragging the photo to reposition it in the frame. This is known as cropping, and is a useful way to compose a better version of your image by selecting the most attractive area.

PHOTOGRAPHY FOR INSTAGRAMMERS

Being a photo-sharing site, Instagram features a very high standard of images. It can take a lifetime to master the art of photography, but simply understanding a few of the basic terms and techniques will help you keep up with the leading Instagrammers. Here's a quickfire guide, applicable to camera or smartphone.

FOCUS

Controlling which parts of your image are sharp, or in focus, is a fundamental technique. On a digital camera you need to master autofocus or manual focus so that you can make your subject pin-sharp. On a smartphone camera, you can use the focus square or circle on your screen—tap the screen on the object you want in focus, and the focus area will move to that point.

EXPOSURE

Exposing an image correctly is about finding the right balance of light—too dark (underexposed) and your subject won't stand out, too light (overexposed) and it becomes too pale and loses detail. Use the metering points on your camera to select your subject—or an area that is midway between the darkest and lightest part of the scene—to get the best exposure. On your smartphone, use the focus point to select the part of the image you want to be exposed correctly.

LIGHT

The best photographers spend a lot of time looking for the best light, which is often at the start or end of the day, around dawn and dusk—known as the "golden hours." It's worth making the effort to get up early or stay out late, as the light during these times adds an attractive warmth to a scene. Adding flash or other artificial lighting to your scene can achieve a world of different effects, and is a key part of studio techniques that can take a lifetime to master.

SHUTTER SPEED

This is the length of the exposure—the time the shutter is open and the sensor is exposed to the image. In darker scenes, you need to allow more light in by using a slower shutter speed to increase the length of exposure. You can also increase the sensitivity of your camera's digital sensor by increasing the ISO, meaning that less light is required. Understanding these basics can help you to be more creative with your photography. For example, using slow shutter speeds will allow movement to blur, while faster shutter speeds will freeze action shots.

APERTURE

The aperture is the opening in a lens, through which light passes. Using a small aperture setting (such as f/11–f/22) will result in a large portion of the scene in front of you appearing in focus, which is useful for landscapes, when you want all of the scene to be sharp. Conversely, using a large aperture setting (in the range f/2–f/8) will mean that only a small part of the scene appears in focus, while the rest is blurred. This is ideal for emphasizing your subject or even just a detail of your subject.

COMPOSITION

Learning the basics of composition can transform your photography. For example, you can use the Rule of Thirds (you can select a thirds grid overlay in your camera or smartphone camera settings menu) and frame your images so the main subject is not dead center but instead aligned with the intersection of two of the thirds gridlines. Another tip is never to shoot a landscape or seascape with the horizon dead center. Positioning your subjects at different points in the frame controls your composition.

LEADING LINES

Another basic approach to successful composition is to look for lines in the scene in front of you—a road, a river, or steps, for instance—that usually start at or toward the bottom of the image and lead off into the distance or around the photo. The lines can be straight or curved. Framing these lines carefully—from front to back, or from one or both corners into the frame—so that they lead into the image, helps to lead the viewer's eye into and around the image, and holds their interest.

PLANNING YOUR INSTAGRAM FEED

Images appear in a Feed as a grid of square images (whatever the shape of your original image), three across. How this grid looks overall is an important part of your "brand," so give some thought to how you want your Feed to look. For instance, do you want to use the same or similar filter for all of your images, or create a checkerboard pattern in which photographs alternate with squares of text? Developing your photography and your Instagram to the point where you have a recognizable style is a true mark of success. Whatever your approach, it helps to plan what you're going to post when—so you don't leave it too long between posts.

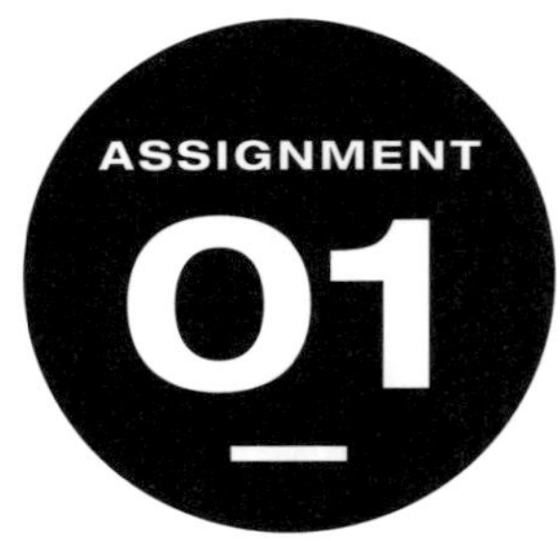

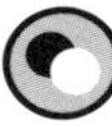

TECHNIQUE

When: For every photo, make sure you've got it in your phone's photo Feed (either by shooting using your phone's camera app or copying from another device).

How:
- Open Instagram.

- Press the + button to start the process.

- Follow the steps on the following pages (don't forget to edit).

- Tap "share" to make your post.

TAGS

It depends on the image, but don't forget to tag the location, your subject, and any photographic style you've used.

MAXIMIZE YOUR POST

Downloading Instagram and posting your first photograph is the start of a creative journey, with you very much in charge of the twists and turns that journey takes. This assignment is designed to ensure that you make best use of all the app's features every time you post a picture to your photo Feed.

Instagram guides you clearly through the posting process so you can do everything in a logical order, and places emphasis on those aspects that help Instagram to provide a good service. To get the most from your image, remember that you can use the full range of image-editing tools available in the app. Follow the step-by-step guide to posting an image on Instagram on pages 14–15 to check that you're not missing any of the key features.

Once you have completed posting an image, you don't have many options. The only way to correct a mistake is to delete the image and start again, losing any Likes you may have earned as well as the position in your Feed (some users like to keep their Feeds chronological). If people have already linked to your post or friends/followers have had a notification to view it, that link will no longer work.

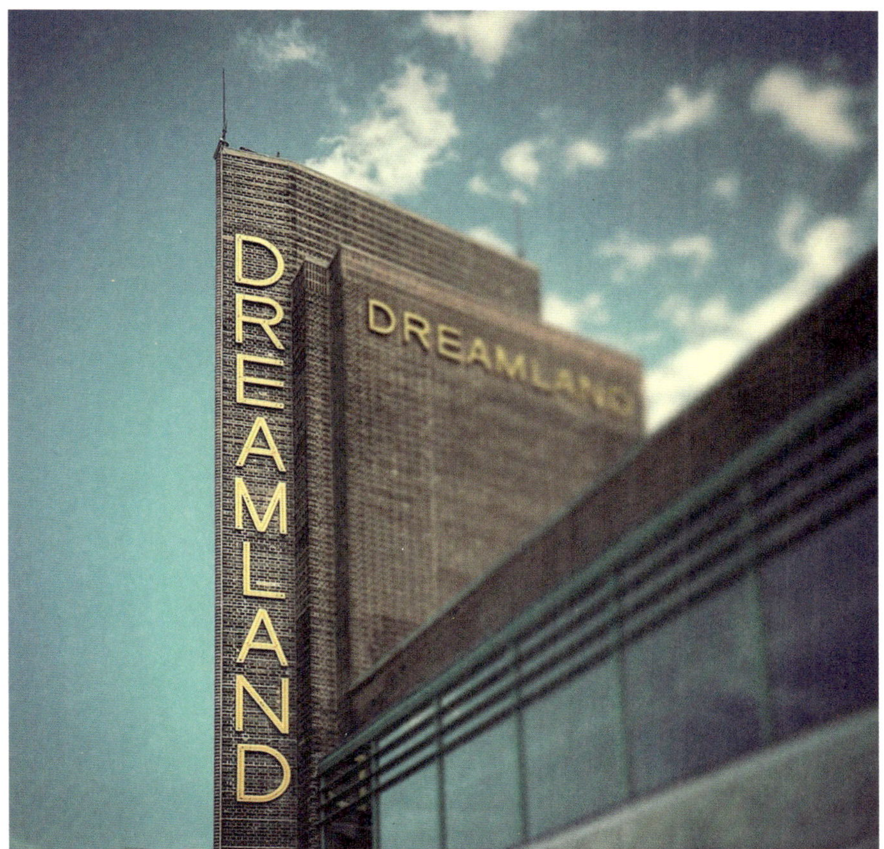

▲ *This photograph of Dreamland in Margate, England, required a little work before it was ready to post to Instagram. The step-by-step on the following pages examines the processes I went through.*

Adam Juniper
@juniperific

TIPS

- In this book we'll suggest hashtags (such as #cat) to help you find and share themes, subjects, and styles using Instagram's search system.

- If hashtags (#) are new to you, pay attention to which ones other people are using.

- Remember that if you tap on a hashtag you will be able to see how many people have posted using that hashtag.

CREATING A POST

These steps guide you through the basic process of selecting an image, making adjustments to it, captioning it, choosing hashtags, and then posting your photograph on Instagram.

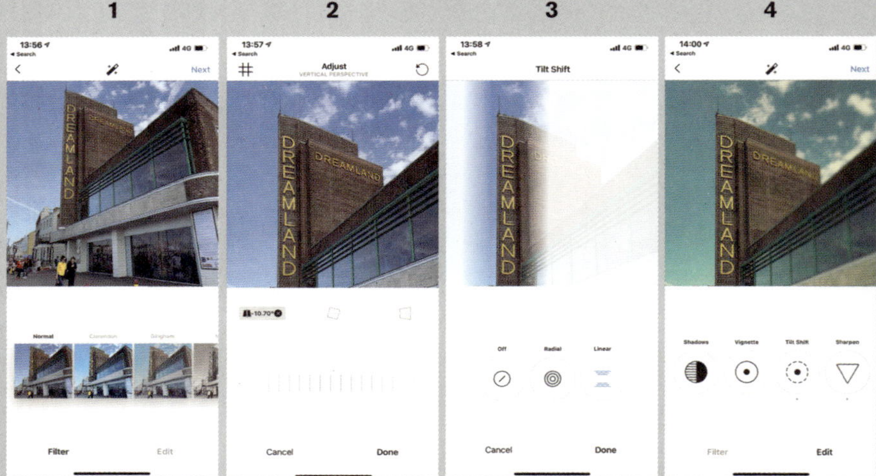

1 When you've chosen the picture you want to post you will be invited to select Filter. Many people only ever select the preset filters, but don't forget that there is an Edit option there, too. You can also pinch and zoom the image on this page to crop it, and drag it so that you see the framing you want, but you'll lose detail if you zoom in too much.

2 For an architectural shot like this, Perspective Correction (you can find this when you select Edit) offers the chance to fix vertical or horizontal perspective—usually the former if you're looking up at a building. Swipe left or right on the slider to adjust the effect and take advantage of the on-screen guides.

3 When you are finished with one correction, tap Done to go back to the other options. In this image, I adjusted the Sharpness to make the bricks stand out, then added a Linear Tilt Shift effect so that only the sign appears in focus. You can move the affected area with your fingers.

4 With the core edits made to the image, I went back to the Filter page and found I liked Maven, but that also made me want to make further edits. So, with the filter applied, I went back to Edit and added a Vignette (which darkens the edges to simulate a poor lens), and tweaked the Brightness and Structure (a little like Sharpness).

5   6   7   8

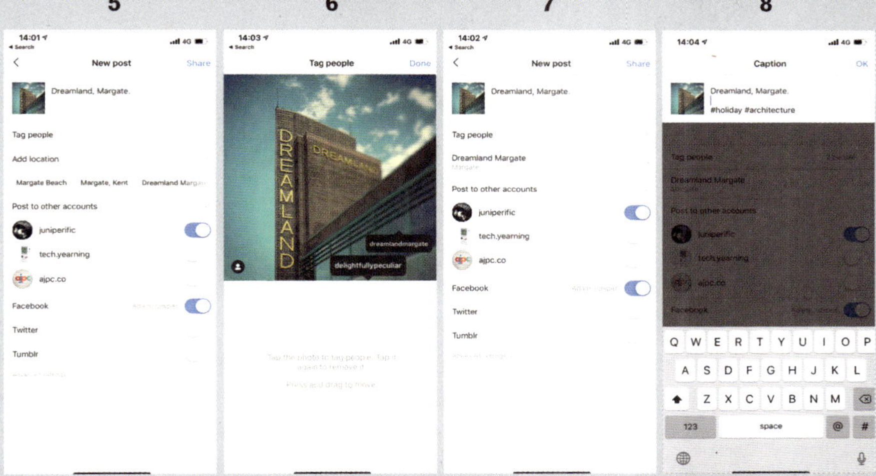

5 When the picture looks right, choose Next and proceed to the Captioning page. In most cases, it helps to give a succinct caption. Think of something that will draw people in immediately, as not all your text will appear unless people click through to the image.

6 Beneath the caption is the Tag People option. This allows you to choose people who are in your image by searching their name. It's always best to include other people who are in your photograph because they'll be alerted to it and will hopefully Like it! You can also include pertinent Instagram accounts—in this case @delightfullypeculiar (who is standing just out of shot) and Dreamland's social media account.

7 If your photograph has GPS location information, choose one of the location suggestions that Instagram offers. If not, you can still search for a location, which again helps you find more potential followers.

8 This is the point at which I go back to the caption to add hashtags. Personally, I find it helps to have dealt with the Location and People fields already, as they can help inspire you to think of related tags—you're allowed up to 30. Look for local Instagrammers (or "igers") groups, too. Finally, select any additional accounts or services you want to post to, check your spelling, and choose Share.

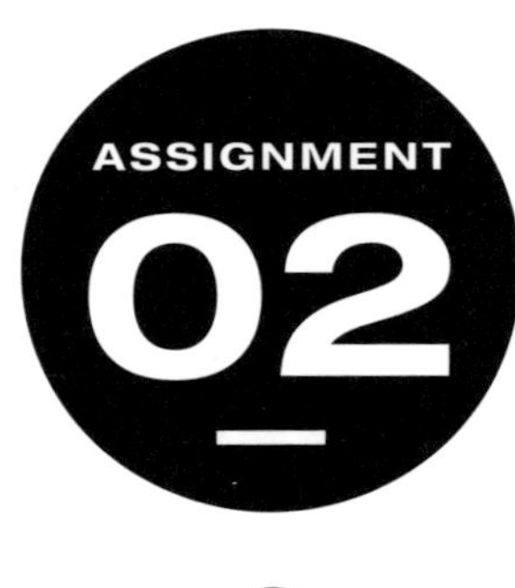

ASSIGNMENT

02

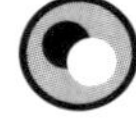

▶ *The examples of Instagram filters shown opposite and on pages 18–19 are just a small selection of the many and ever-changing options.*

Jason Hook
@jasonhookbooks

TECHNIQUE

When: After shooting, applying a filter is part of the sharing process (choose Normal to avoid applying one).

How: After you choose a photo, you'll see the filters. Scroll left and right to choose from the preview. Tap the preview again to adjust the strength. Choose Edit or Next to continue.

Filters: Many and varied.

TAGS

Some Instagrammers tag with the filter's name, but this can be confusing—Gingham, for example, is a fabric pattern too, so the sewing community will view the search differently.

FILTER TIPS

When they wanted to add an effect to individual photo, traditional photographers had to alter the image "in camera" or in the darkroom. Home developing in a darkroom was not available to everyone, but placing a filter over the camera lens allowed different colors or tones—even gradients—to be achieved. You had to carry the filter in your bag, and it took a few moments to screw it on. By planning ahead, a photographer could also influence a photo's final appearance by choosing a particular type of film. Every photo on a roll of 24 or 36 pictures would have to use the same effect, but there were awesome looks to be had, not to mention the choice of color or black and white. One type of film, Kodachrome, had such distinctive rich, saturated colors that National Geographic insisted all its photographers use it.

Instagram borrows the word "filter" from traditional photography but applies it to a broader range of possibilities, effectively including the tonal variations from different types of film, simulations of the texture from different processing methods, and effects somewhat like an optical filter. Despite the name, Instagram filters are closer to what most photographers would call a "preset." Because they are simulations, not hard pieces of optical glass, you can adjust the strength of their effect on a scale of 0–100: just tap a second time on the filter you have selected and drag the slider.

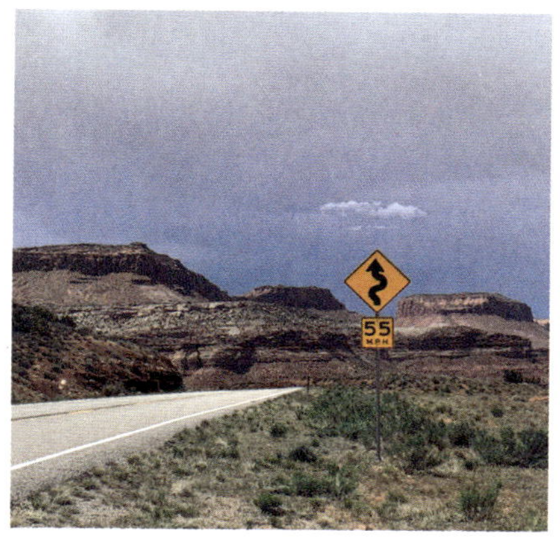

NO FILTER

▲ *The photograph as imported by Instagram. Strictly speaking, a number of digital effects might well have been applied, either by your camera (which, after all, is a kind of computer), or an app outside Instagram.*

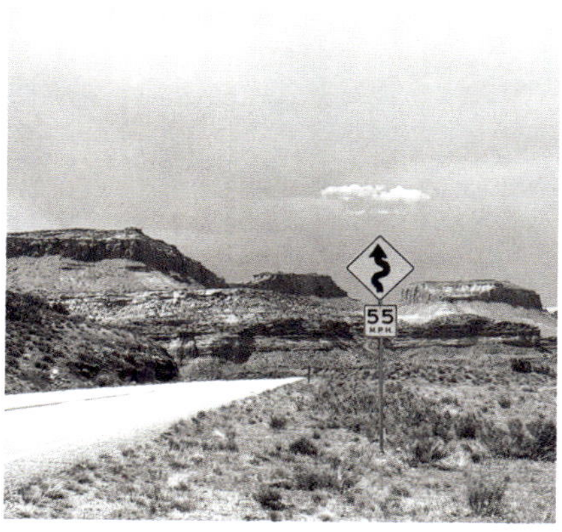

INKWELL

▲ *The most simple black-and-white effect in Instagram; it doesn't especially exaggerate tone, so landscapes may be flat, but it's a good filter for portraits.*

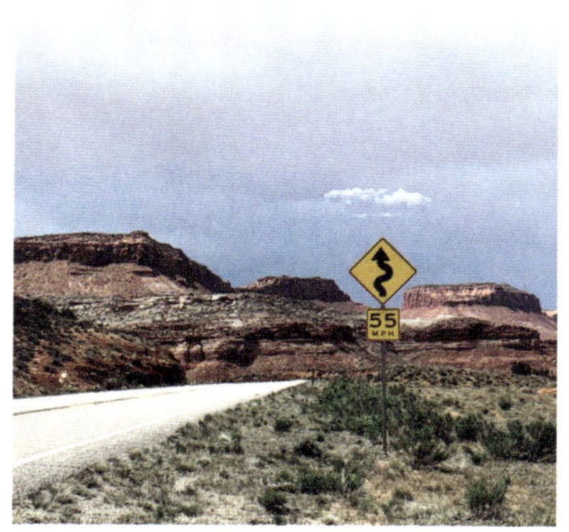

JUNO

▲ *Enhances red and yellow areas, perfect for the grungy, hipster, urban look (some might say "authentic," without fully appreciating the irony in photographic terms).*

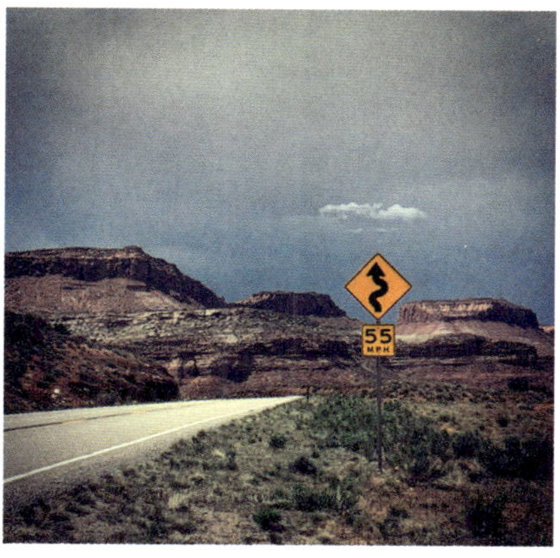

X-PRO II

▲ *The filter's name is a reference to cross-processed film. As well as adding a strong vignette that darkens corners, it pushes up the contrast and works best on fairly bright images.*

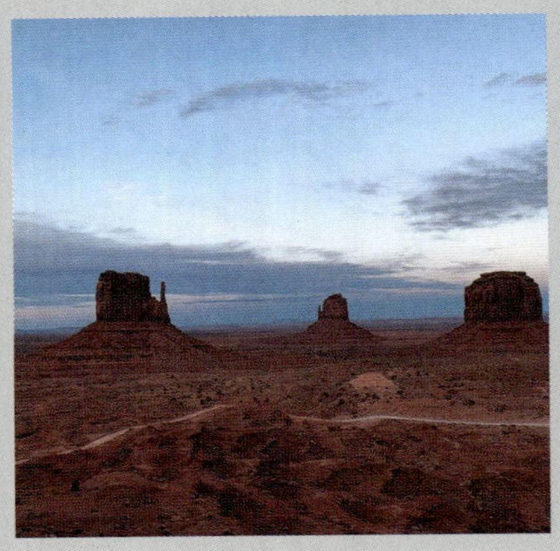

NO FILTER

▲ *An iPhone photograph of Monument Valley Navajo Tribal Park, USA, as imported by Instagram. If you wish to add a filter, there is a small selection shown here, but you should experiment to find your style.*

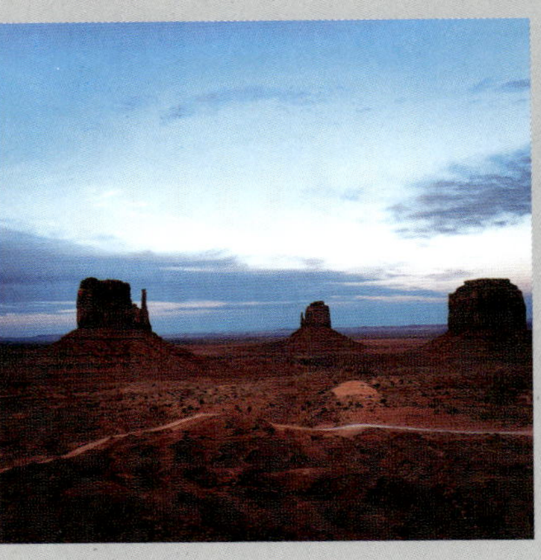

LO-FI

▲ *This filter darkens already dark areas, and boosts color saturation. It is better on things than people, and is a popular filter for food photographers.*

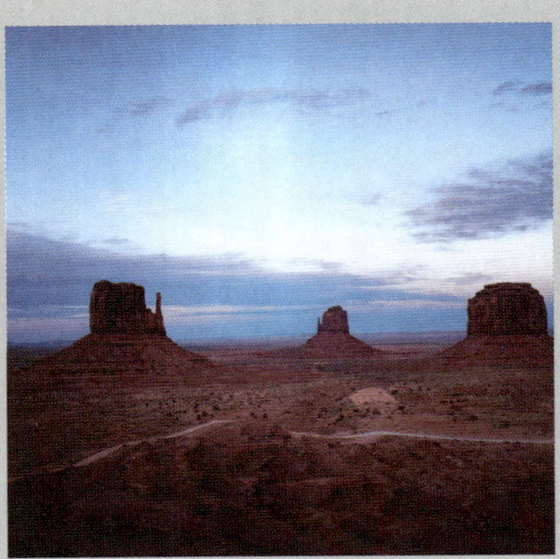

LARK

▲ *Good for nature, hikes, and the outdoors, the Lark filter boosts the green and blue ends of the spectrum, keeping colors cool.*

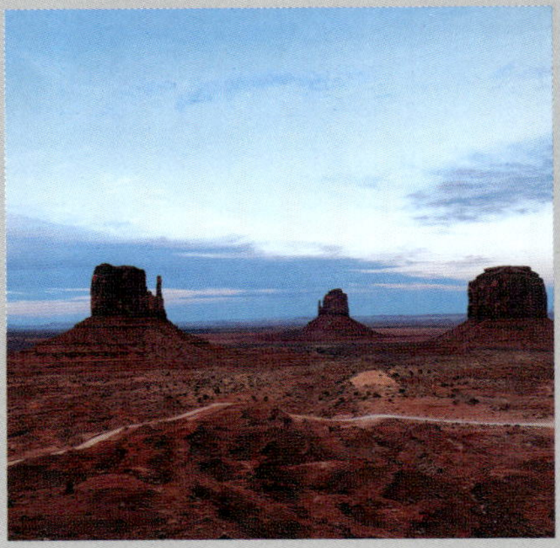

CLARENDON

▲ *A popular—perhaps over-used—contrast booster, which is the natural choice for sunset shots. It brightens all bright areas and darkens shadows.*

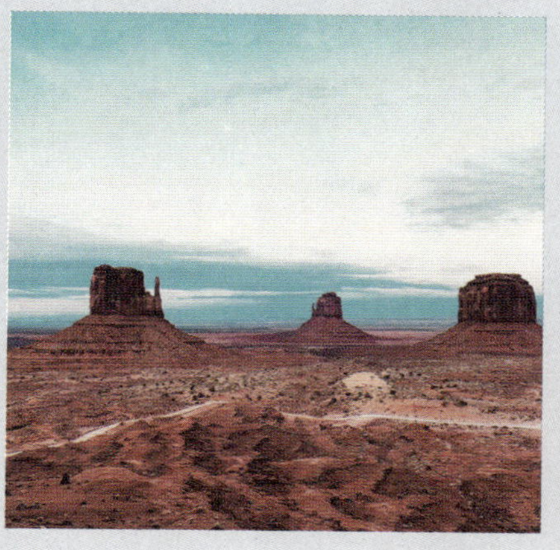
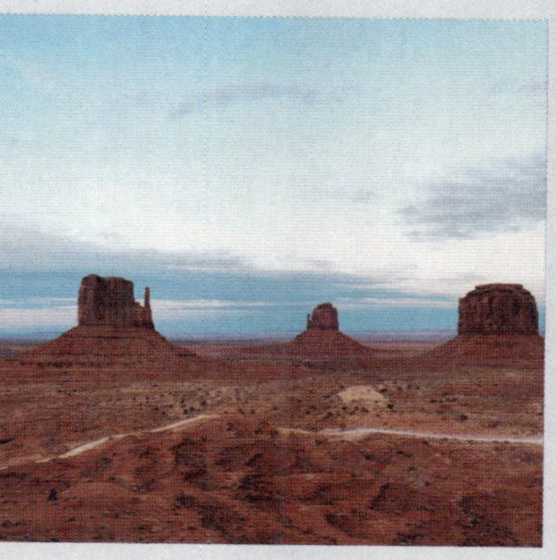

REYES

▲ *A curious combination of desaturation and brightening for a washed out look, also giving something of a retro look (a lot like Gingham).*

GINGHAM

▲ *A color retro look, which takes color away to give the impression of washed-out vacation photos, or of calm selfies.*

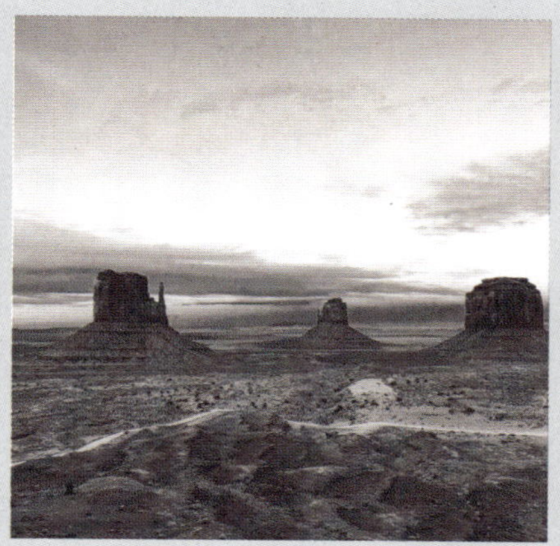
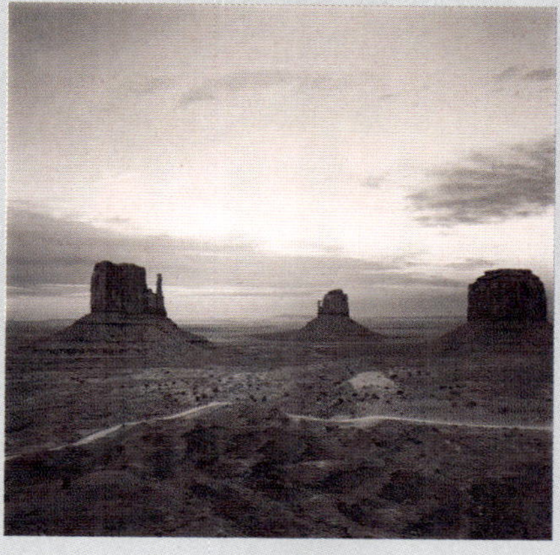

MOON

▲ *A black-and-white filter, which darkens dark areas. It will add contrast to most skin tones, and is also good for portraits.*

WILLOW

▲ *A black-and-white filter with relatively low contrast, which can make even bad shots look good. For selfie fans, give it a try to rescue a bad-hair day.*

TECHNIQUE

When: This is a great technique to keep in mind for any image that features strong colors.

Where: Especially useful in travel photography, when capturing interesting places.

How: To make best use of the principle of opposing colors, all you need to do is commit the color wheel to memory (sounds weird, but you'll find it happens quite naturally after a while).

Filter: Use Juno to make colors really "pop," or increase Contrast and Brightness.

TAGS

#color #colour #colorful #colourful #contrast

Also mention specific key colors that are dominant in your image: #blue #yellow

COLOR YOUR INSTA

This is a technical assignment based around the color wheel and the application of the principle of opposing colors on the wheel to create pleasing tones in your images. You can also use these principles in curating your Feed itself.

In some programs on your computer, when you're trying to pick a jaunty tone for that headline font, you'll find the color tones are represented by a wheel. That isn't just a nice idea the programmers came up with—it's something that artists have been using for hundreds of years. Essentially, every color has an opposite, which appears on the opposite side of the color wheel. These pairings generally contrast well. Red opposes cyan, yellow opposes blue, and green opposes magenta.

There are subtle variations. You can, for example, create an equilateral triangle to find three hues that work together (triadic colors—see overleaf), and explore color theory in as much detail as you like. But the simple opposites are easy to remember and apply in your day-to-day photography and Instagram posts.

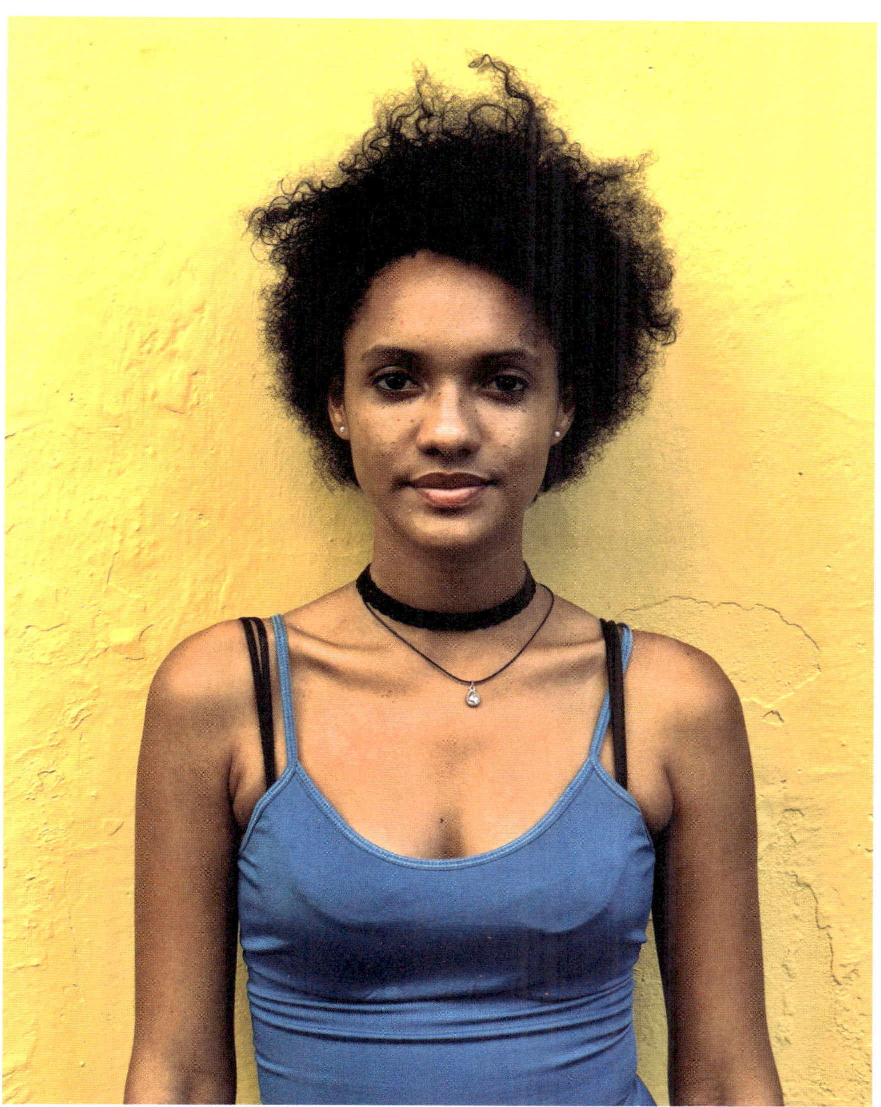

▲ *This vibrant portrait makes good use of the contrasting colors—more effective as the bright blue and yellow are on opposite sides of the color wheel.*

Jack Hollingsworth
@jackhollingsworth

ROLLING THE COLOR WHEEL

The examples here show exactly how the hues in different groups counter and complement each other. From a photography perspective, keep them in mind, but don't be bound by them. You can also use black-and-white filters if you're struggling to get nice color shades in a scene.

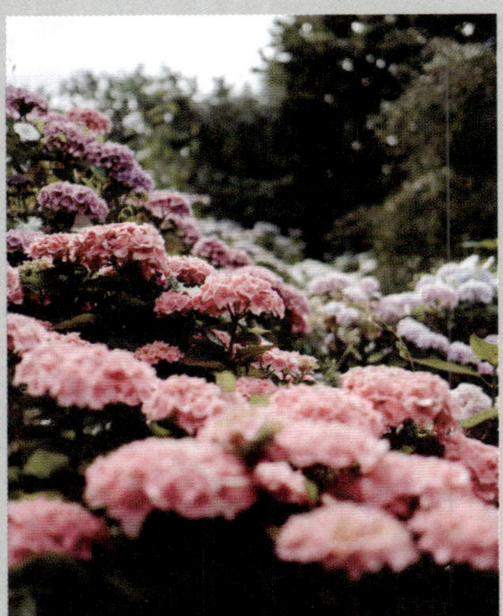

◄ COMPLEMENTARY

This is the simple principle of using hues that are opposite each other on the color wheel. You'll note that it doesn't matter that the hues are darker or lighter—it's the pure hue that is important, although in practice highly saturated shades do work well in Instagram.

Annie Spratt
@anniespratt

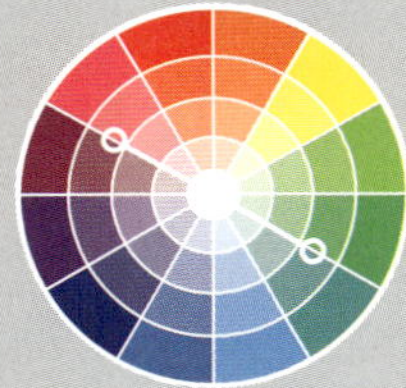

ANALOGOUS ►

Take the analogous approach by seeking hues that are near to each other on the color wheel but about the same level of brightness or darkness.

Aziz Acharkl
@aziz_acharki

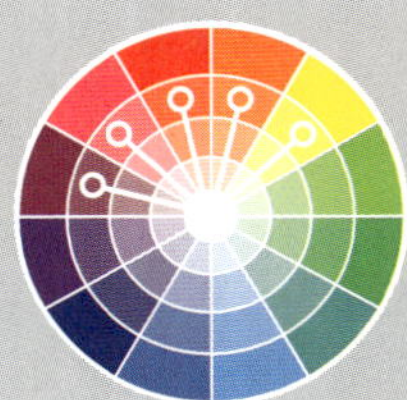

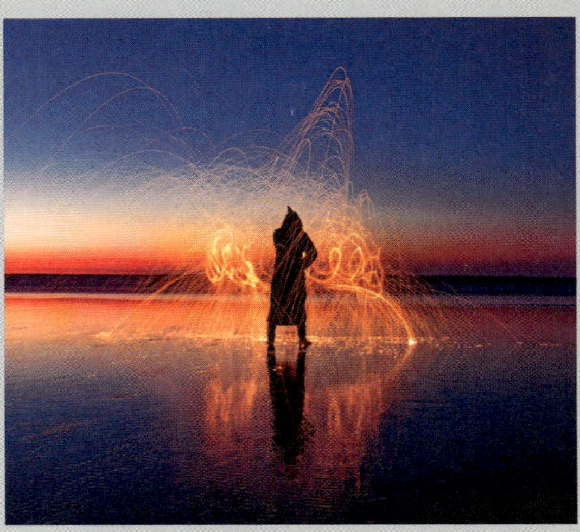

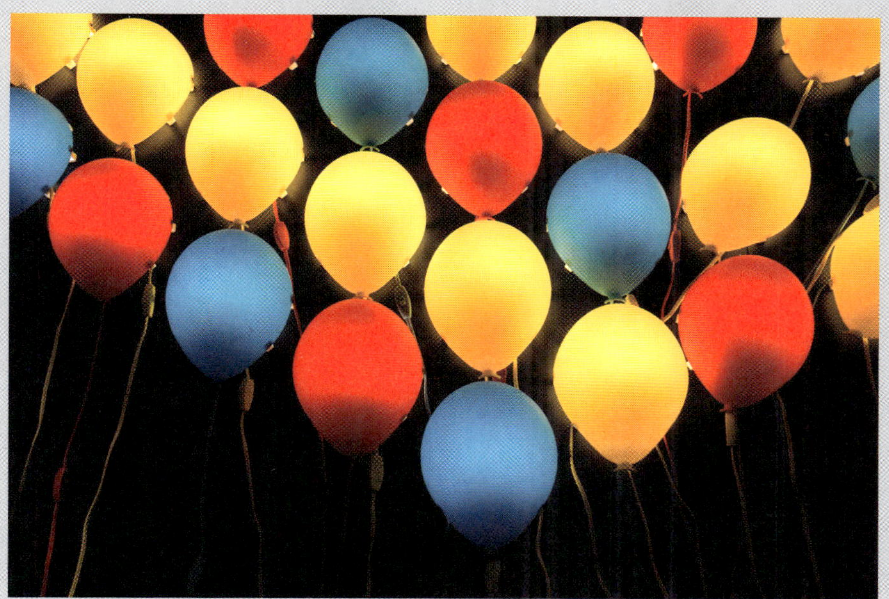

TRIADIC ▲

This is a similar approach to the complementary principle, but here three colors are evenly spaced, each a third of the way around the color wheel. The three colors need to be carefully matched—one usually dominates the other two.

Jason Leung
@xninjason

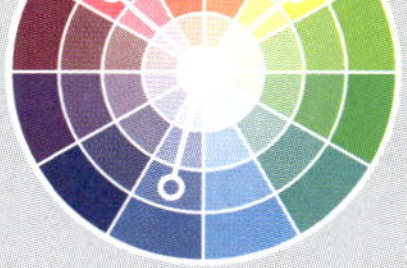

SINGLE ▶

An alternative way to use color is to look for images that don't stray outside one shade. Obviously, this doesn't fit the opposing colors assignment, but it's another approach to thinking about color that can illuminate your Instagram.

Mei Ying
@meiyingmeiying

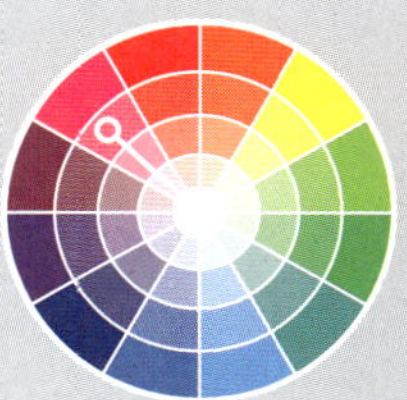

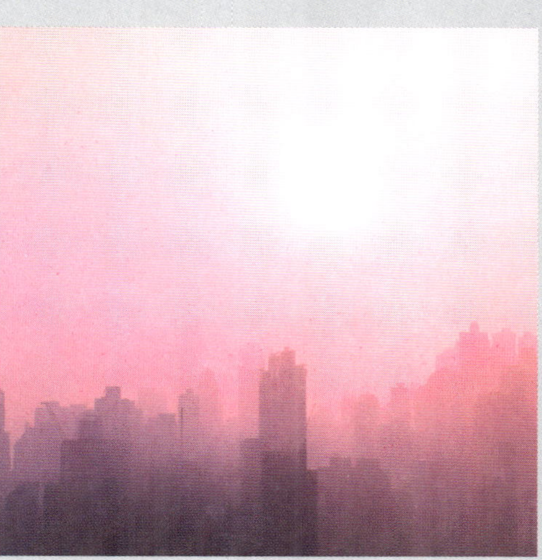

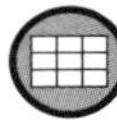

TECHNIQUE

When: Every time you post (make sure the photo you want is on your smartphone).

How: Experiment with the Edit functions in Instagram, by adjusting the Brightness and Contrast, converting to black and white, or adding a frame or vignette, for example. There are also many editing apps that will alter the look of your image.

TAGS

These depend on your image, but remember to include location, subject, and any photographic style you've used.

ENHANCE YOUR IMAGE

Taking great smartphone images doesn't stop with pressing the touchscreen button and uploading them straight to Instagram. Good editing can be the difference between a flat, lifeless representation and a vibrant, moody masterpiece. Your creative brief for this assignment is simply to explore the editing possibilities for your images in a little more depth. Editing software has improved in leaps and bounds over the past few years, and Instagram offers a selection of adjustment controls that are capable of transforming average photographs into something quite wonderful.

You can use the preset filters that come with the app, but there are also many ways in which you can manually edit your images to ensure a much more polished end product. As with traditional photography, it is not uncommon for professional smartphone photographers to spend as much time editing their images as they do composing the shot.

You can experiment with a number of different editing applications. All smartphones include in-depth, picture-editing software that allows you to tweak and adjust your images. There are hundreds of third-party apps, too, from the very simple to highly creative and sophisticated products such as Snapseed and Photoshop Elements. And don't forget to skip the preset filters and try your hand at fine-tuning your images via the in-app editing steps.

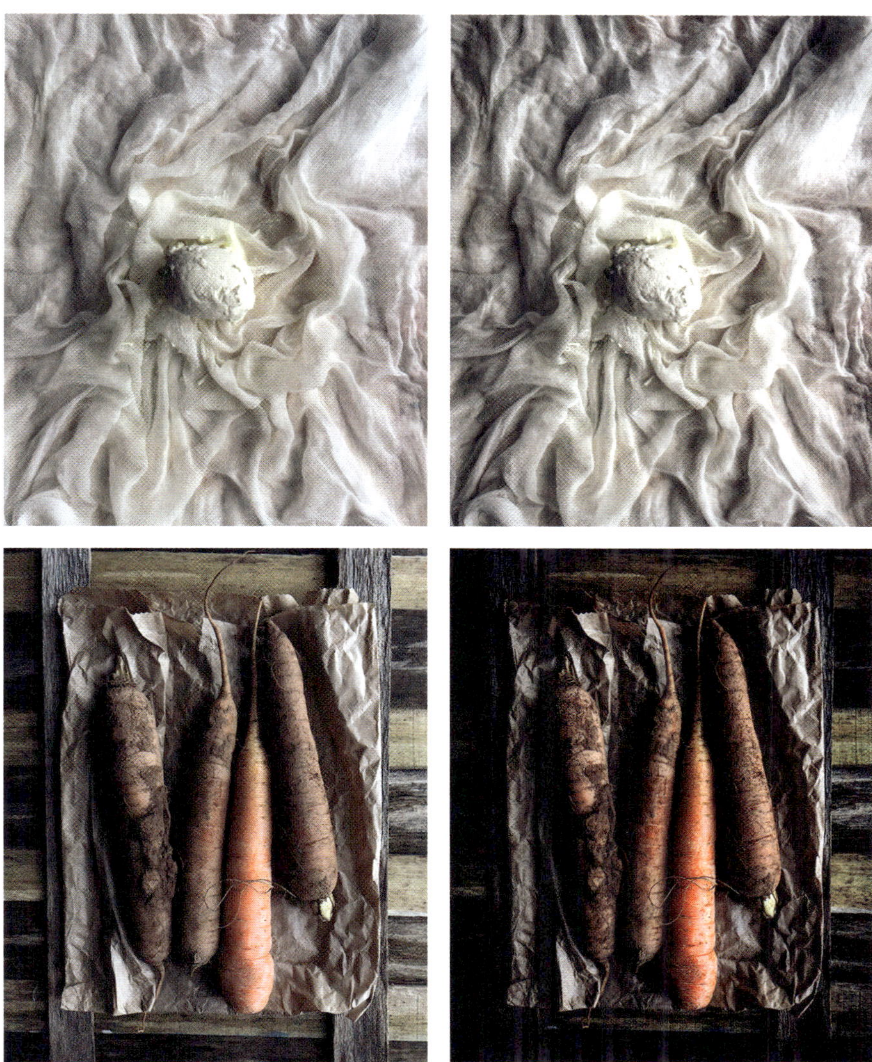

▲ *Two examples of strong images (left) that have been enhanced (right) through the editing features of Instagram. The top-right image of the soft cheese, labneh, has simply had tweaks to shadows and highlights to accentuate the drama of the muslin sheet that has been unwrapped from around the cheese. The carrots have had alterations to highlights and shadows, too, plus a boost to saturation and a vignette effect added to the edge of the frame. The final image is stronger and less flat. There is an almost tangible richness.*

Matt Inwood
@matt_inwood

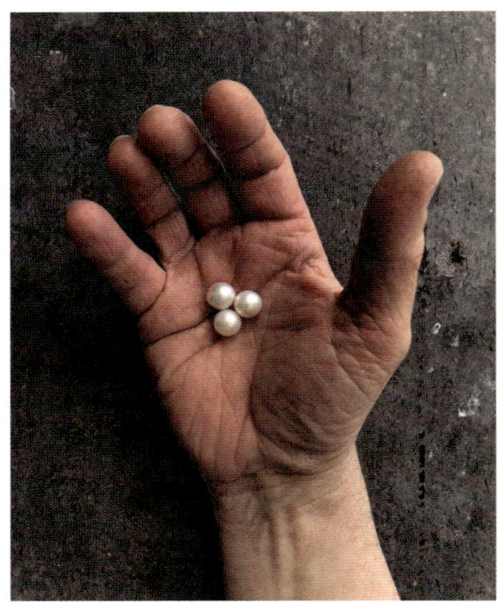

There's no set sequence to editing your images, but you should always look to
correct any deficient elements of the image first and progress from there. For
instance, it might be that the image is a little too dark and needs the shadows or
brightness lifting. Sometimes the image might be a little too blue (when shooting
with light late in the day, perhaps), so you should aim to increase the Warmth in
order to counterbalance this. Images created in artificially lit places such as bars
and restaurants can have an orange cast to them—you can reduce the Warmth and
neutralize the orange by adding a cooler hue.

Work your way systematically through the Edit controls, adjusting anything that you
feel could enhance your photo, but don't fall into the trap of editing for editing's sake.
Watch carefully what you're doing: you should be trying to refine and enhance rather
than creating and filtering something from scratch. Taking time to carefully edit your
images can really transform your photo from an average shot to something that will
grab the attention of your followers.

Beyond correcting flaws, editing your images with care can add drama to a portrait,
perhaps by accentuating shadows and adding vignette shading to the edges of the
frame. Contrast, Sharpen, and Structure tools can crisp up detail and really make
things "pop." And desaturating an image or removing color altogether can transform
a portrait into something with real mood and gravitas.

Take time to edit your image before you post it, and you will start to see this
assignment really bear fruit in your Feed.

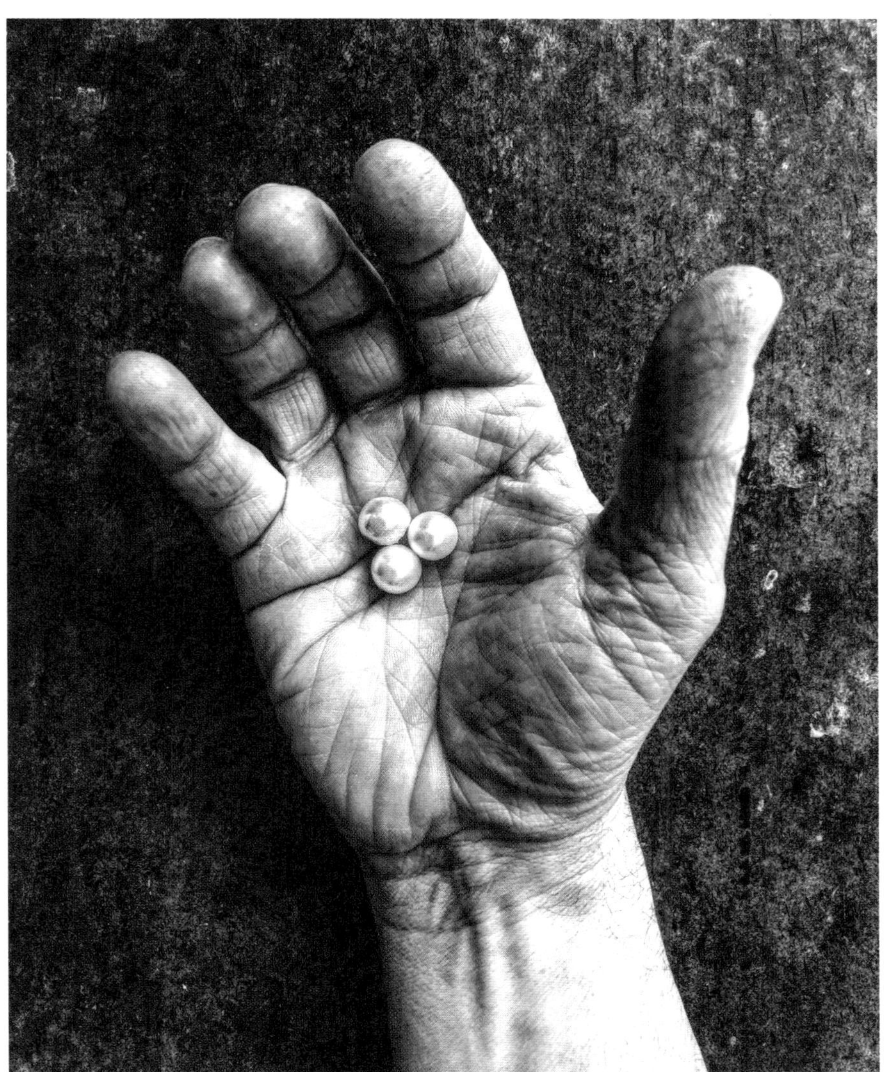

▲ *An image of a jeweler's hand, holding three pearls in the palm. The original image (opposite) doesn't inspire much, but the edited image (above)—devoid of color, and with shadows, contrast, and structure all greatly enhanced—becomes something much more striking and powerful. The hand now dwarfs the pearls. Each line and shadow on the palm speaks of the maker and craftsman that they belong to, capturing both the power and finesse in that hand. The pearls remain delicate and treasure-like at the center of the frame.*

Matt Inwood
@matt_inwood

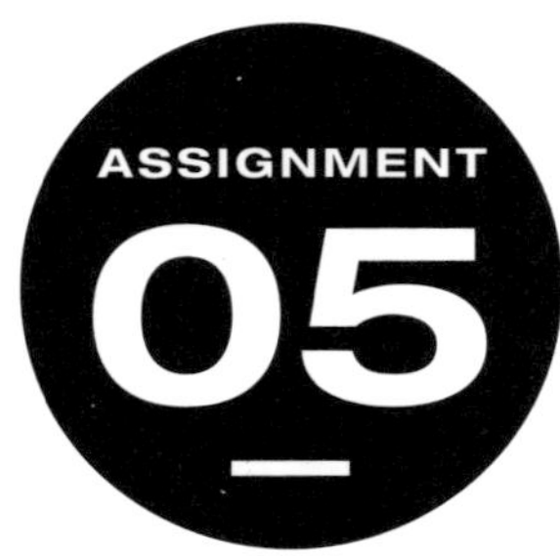

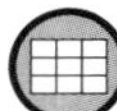
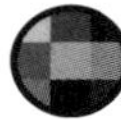

TECHNIQUE

When: Let the light be your filter, and aim to shoot at sunrise or sunset.

Where: Landscapes or cityscapes with clear skylines are good.

How: Simply post a photograph without using filters. This means you need to concentrate on shooting in good light to get the image right.

Filter: None this time!

TAGS

#nofilter #nofilterneeded #shotoniphone #igersbirmingham ("igers" is the common short form for "Instagrammers") #architecture_hunter

#NOFILTER

Instagrammers tend to have a preference for using their own language of filters, significantly altering how an image looks, and often fitting their own particular style or brand. So widespread is this craze for filters that it's generated its own backlash. The #nofilter hashtag has taken off in response, and aims to encourage the sharing of scenes that are too beautiful to need manipulation. Some posters also use it to compliment the beauty of a human subject.

For this assignment, your brief is to find an everyday scene—a landscape or cityscape— and capture it in such good lighting that manipulation is unnecessary. It's worth remembering that most cameras, especially those on smartphones, are always doing a little work to help you create a good photograph—that's just the technology at work. But the goal here is simply to stick to the Normal option on Instagram's Filter page, and create a great image that avoids the artificial look.

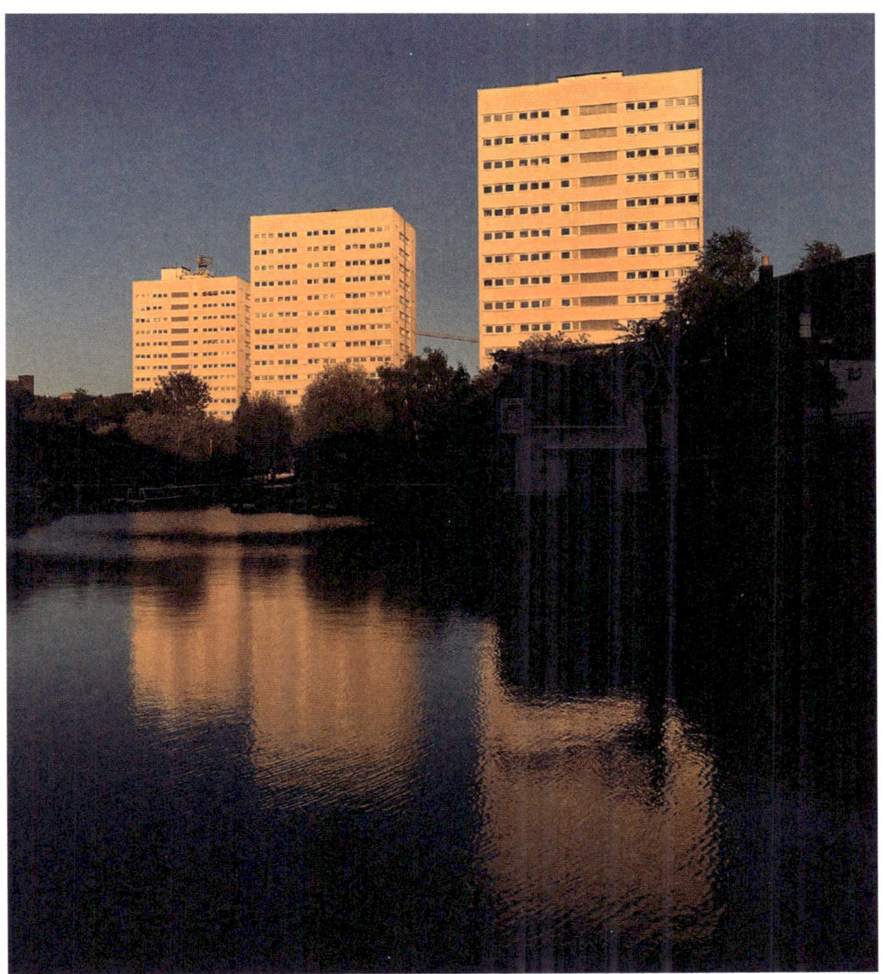

▲ *This iPhone capture by award-winning architecture photographer Tim Cornbill shows how some unprepossessing apartment blocks can still look good in the right light.*

Tim Cornbill
@timcornbill

ASSIGNMENT JOURNAL

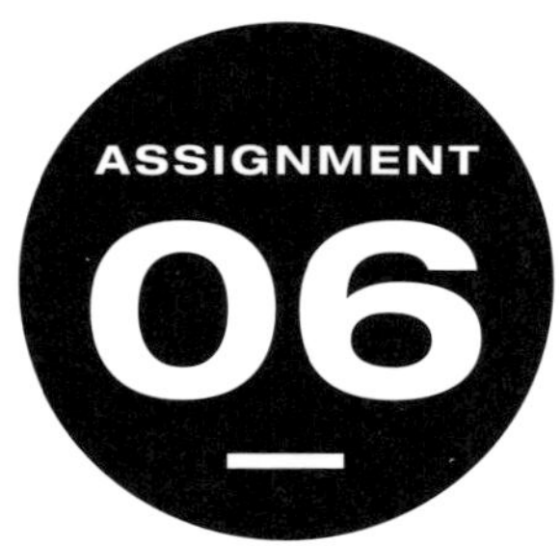

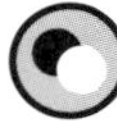
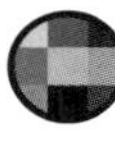
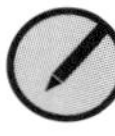

TECHNIQUE

When: Important moments can be anything from a new product to—for a small business—changing your coffee mug.

Where: Unless the location is the brand, it's good to mix this up and show you can take your look to more than one place.

How: Find a consistent color palette, style, and composition in your images to create a distinct personality that is unique to you.

Filters: Go easy here—if you want your brand to have longevity, don't get stuck with a look that might go out of fashion!

TAGS

Make sure you research tags that work for your particular brand/product, plus: #brand #brandambassador

#BRAND

Not long ago, regarding yourself as a personal "brand" was seen by some as a little distasteful and self-important. But the world moves quickly and it's essential today to present yourself on social media in a way that people can digest and identify with. Like it or not, how you portray yourself online is your brand—and the more consistently you do it, the more you'll build recognition, Follower count, and Likes.

There are several ways to build your brand. First, always choose subjects, an object, a color palette, or a style that you like, and which helps to define who you are to people and what you want to show them. Then, when shooting and editing images, always use the same style and filters. Think about the Instagram grid itself when you add your photos, and which photos will look good next to each other. Finally, make sure you write your captions in a consistent tone of voice.

For this assignment, shoot a series of different images with something that unites them visually. If you're just sharing your own news or images, this can simply be your presence in the photographs. If you're a small business, try to show what your business does and—crucially—what sets you apart from your competition.

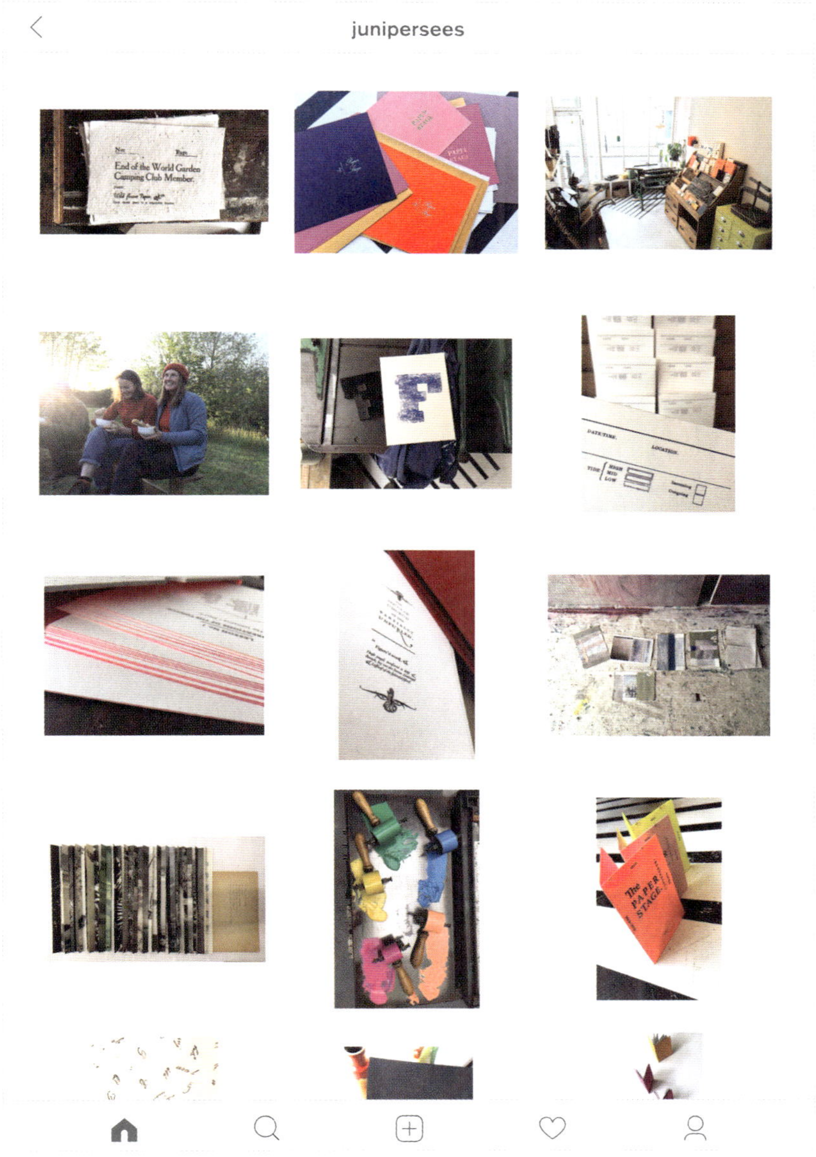

▲ *Running a traditional printing business in trendy Falmouth, in the south-west of England, Emily shares both the product and its story. White borders from the Witagram app, consistent use of natural light, and a broad concentration on products or machinery rather than people, make for a consistent look and strong personality that doesn't feel exclusive.*

Emily Juniper
@junipersees

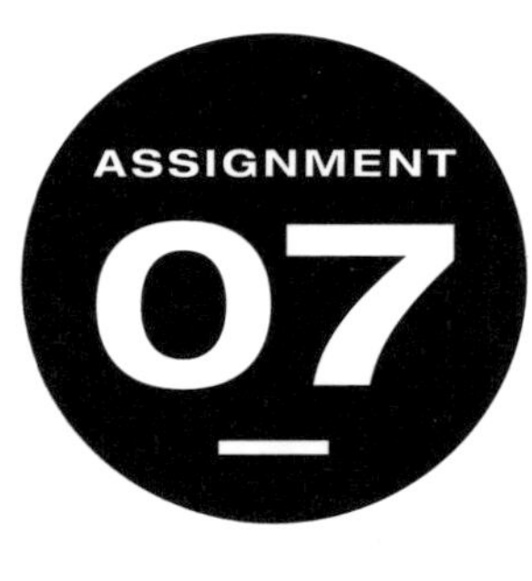

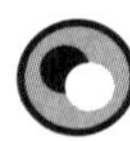
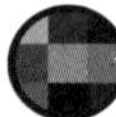
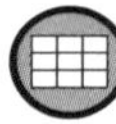

TECHNIQUE

When: Early morning for the best, golden light.

Where: Lakes, mountains, and quiet beaches.

How: Get up early for the light and concentrate on composition, looking for subjects and lines in the scene that will draw the viewer in.

Filter: Mayfair works well with skies, while Sutro is fun on a cloudy day.

TAGS

#wideangle #landscape #landscapephotography #ruleofthirds

THE GREAT OUTDOORS

These days, most of the population lives and works in an urban environment most of the time. More than a few of them will be wistfully wishing they were somewhere else with a little more freedom. So, if you happen to be somewhere like that, in the great outdoors, use it to your Instagram's advantage.

Landscape photographers often use wideangle lenses, and that's exactly what you've got in your smartphone. However, if you need to show more of a scene, see if your smartphone has a built-in panorama mode. See the Tips opposite for some more ideas on how to compose and capture an outdoor landscape that will stand out from the crowd.

Your brief is to head out of town and look to photograph and share aspects of rural or remote life that offer a striking contrast to the urban and suburban world. When shooting landscapes, look for objects in the scene—such as a tree or building—that can act as a focal point, or lines that draw the eye into the image. Outdoor shots don't have to be grand, sweeping landscape views, either. As an alternative, look for details or interesting objects that reflect the character of a place, or features that capture the culture of rural areas.

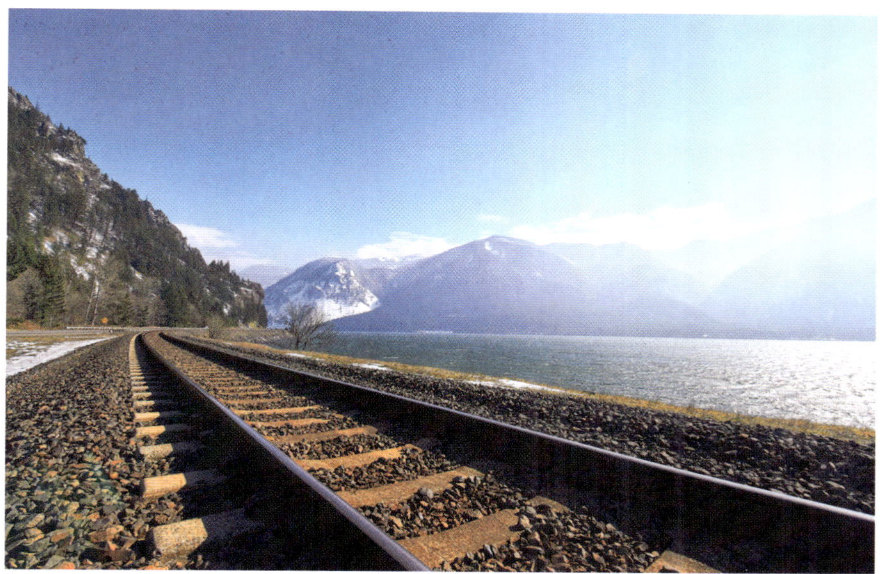

▲ *This shot of the banks of the Columbia River in Washington State, USA, doesn't just show the vastness of the space, it also reveals a perspective that city-dwellers don't get to experience too often. Shooting from low down on the railway tracks means the leading lines of the tracks carry the viewer into the scene.*

Dan M Lee
@danmleephotography

TIPS

- Good light is very important for outdoor photography. About 20-30 minutes before sunrise or sunset—the "golden hours"—often provides the best light of the day.

- Get the exposure right when you shoot the picture (see page 10). Ensure that your image is neither too light nor too dark by using your camera's metering or your smartphone's focus area to select the subject area.

- On a camera, use a small aperture (such as f/20) and focus on a point in the foreground to ensure as much of the image as possible is in focus.

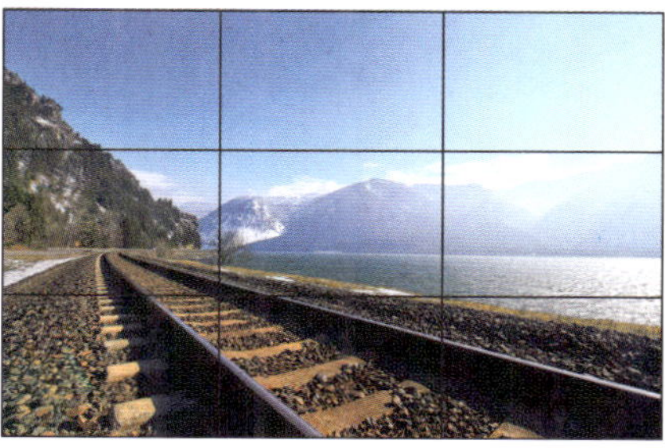

▲ *Compose your image using the Rule of Thirds to help you position objects and lines in the frame. Place your subjects on the points at which the lines intersect.*

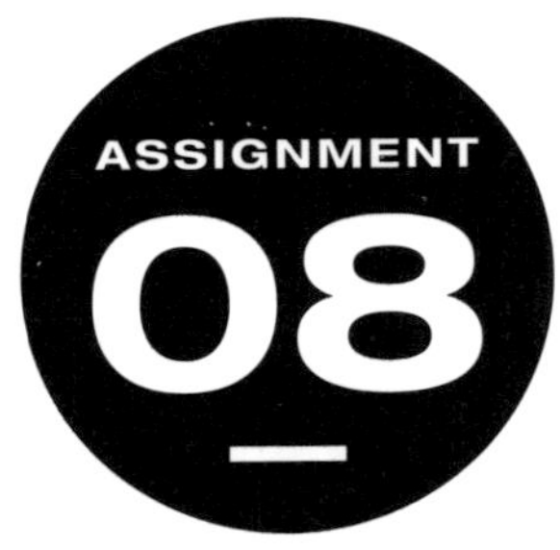

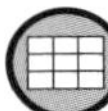

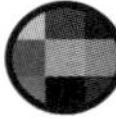

TECHNIQUE

When: Any time of day or night.

Where: Street photography needs an urban environment and usually a human element for context.

How: Zoom to between 1.5x and 2x on a smartphone camera (or find your 50mm lens), and make sure you fill the frame with interesting objects and movement.

TAGS

For street and documentary styles, use #photography, #streetphotography, #streetphoto, and for black-and-white photography add #blackandwhite, #bnw

STREET LIFE

Street photographers like to get close to the action and fill the frame with people, movement, and objects. That means they prefer to use lenses of what is known as a "standard" length (equivalent to 50mm on a 35mm camera). Your smartphone camera is likely to have a focal length more like a wideangle lens (equivalent to 26-33mm on a 35mm camera). This means you will need to get even closer to people, but you can turn this to your advantage. Practicing street photography with a smartphone, you are much more discreet. A phone is a "normal" item for people to be carrying around, and it draws much less attention in a crowd than a chunky camera.

Your brief is to head for the visually interesting parts of town, where there are lots of great subjects: people, storefronts, signs, vehicles, lights, colors, patterns, and movement. Patience is a virtue, and it's often worth watching and waiting for the perfect moment when someone moves into shot. Be aware that in some locations—such as France—photographing strangers in the street without permission is now illegal. Keep safe, don't hassle people, and, if in doubt, ask permission. When you have completed the assignment, post your best four images to Instagram over four days. You should discover that street photography has a huge following.

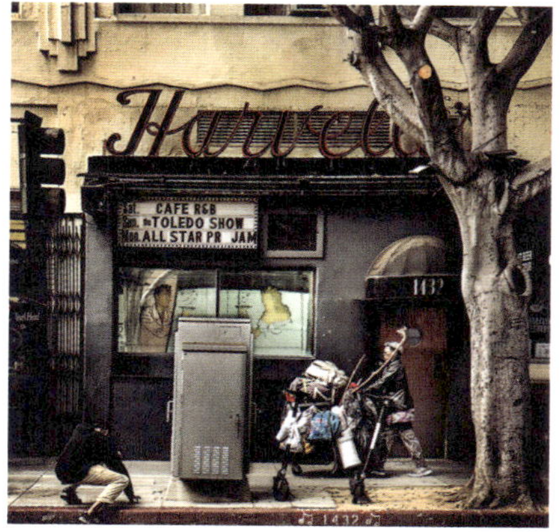

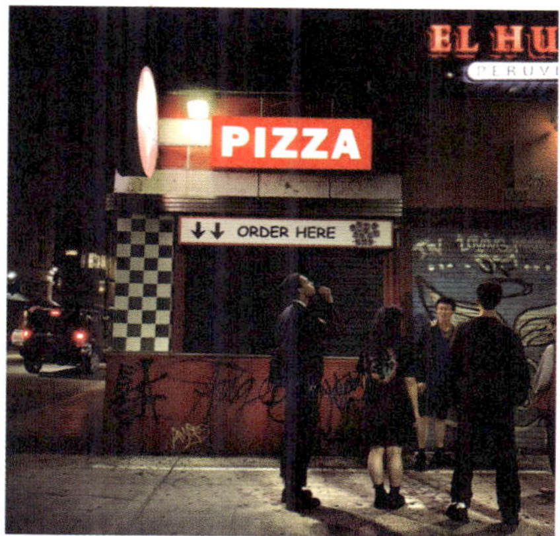

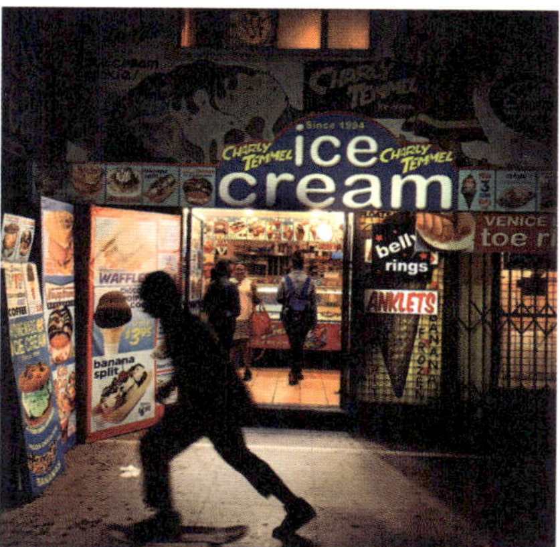

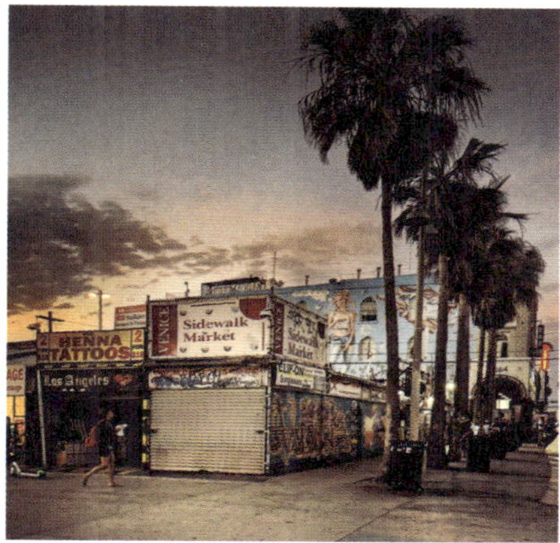

▲ *Sally Davies is a New York-based photographer who has won international acclaim. Taken using her smartphone, her images emphasize the rich colors of the streets. Sally often uses the wideangle field of view of a smartphone to her advantage—in two of these images she has included trees to help frame the shot and add linear structure.*

Sally Davies
@sallydaviesphoto

ASSIGNMENT JOURNAL

TIP

Some smartphones come with a second lens (typically equivalent to 52mm on a 35mm camera), which provides a field of view similar to the cameras and lenses favored by traditional street photographers, such as the legendary Henri Cartier-Bresson.

TECHNIQUE

When: Whenever you have the opportunity to take a planned or impromptu portrait.

Where: Selfies are all about showing off location, outfits, or today's look, so ideally capture them in front of interesting or iconic backgrounds.

How: Shoot a selfie, paying attention to capturing a mood and to using interesting poses and locations.

Filter: Juno or Ludwig for a bit of contrast, but also think about which Filter suits your personality and the "look" you want to give your images.

TAGS

#selfie #selfportrait #pose

#SELFIE

If there's one thing people learn to do these days, in the Age of the Selfie, it's pose for the camera. Instagram needs to be regularly fed with poses, but it's a good idea to keep an open mind about where you grab that shot. For this assignment, your brief is to spend a week simply shooting pictures of yourself, and yourself with your friends, at every available opportunity. Use the tips in the captions opposite to start thinking about different approaches to the selfie, and to portraits in general.

Instagram's underlying programming—or "algorithm"—likes data, so shoot group poses in which you tag friends. This helps the software to work out who your friends are and to make sure they see and Like your photos. This creates a virtuous circle. To widen the circle a little further, you also need an element of surprise—that means it's a good idea to grab the pose somewhere unexpected or unusual.

Many of the most successful Instagram accounts have a special personality to create their "brand." Simply featuring regular self-portraits is one way to create your online personality and presence. But you can strengthen this by posting similar subjects and types of shot, and by using the same filters and "look" for all your images.

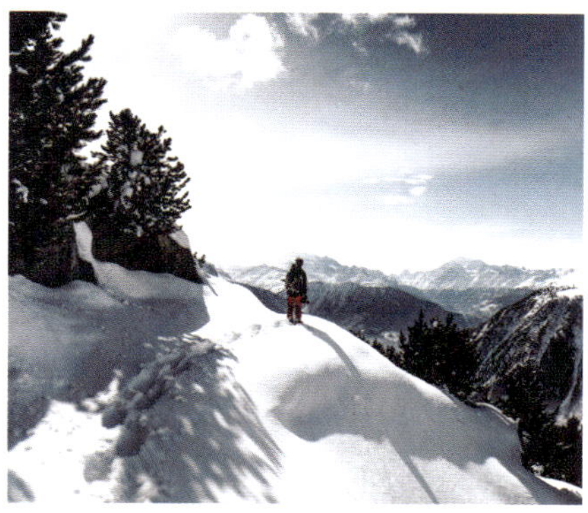

▲ *If you're on your own and want to take a panoramic selfie, use the self-timer on your camera or smartphone. Pre-focus before taking up your position by focusing on something the same distance from the lens.*

Dino Reichmuth
@dino.reichmuth

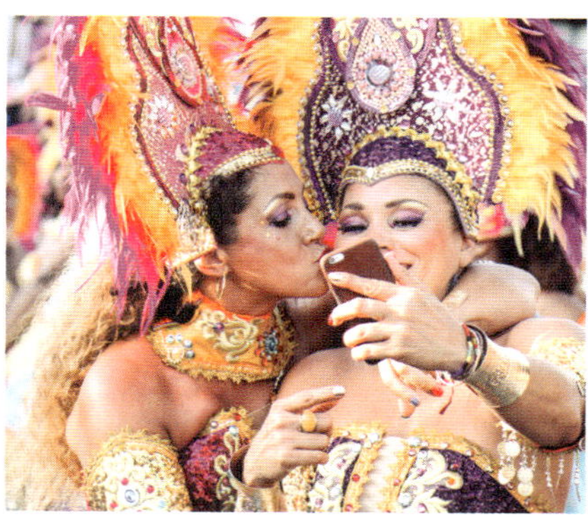

▲ *Sometimes you might have only a few seconds to capture the moment for the best portrait of yourself or others. Experiment with the Burst function, which takes lots of images so that you can then select the best one.*

Quinten de Graaf
@quinten_and_more

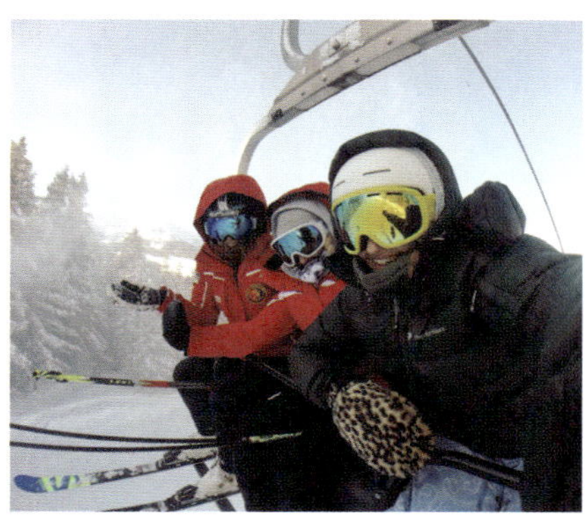

▲ *Frame your shot carefully. Be aware of your surroundings, what's in the background, what you choose to include, and what you choose to crop out. This will help to ensure your image is full of interest.*

Emma Paillex
@emma.paillex

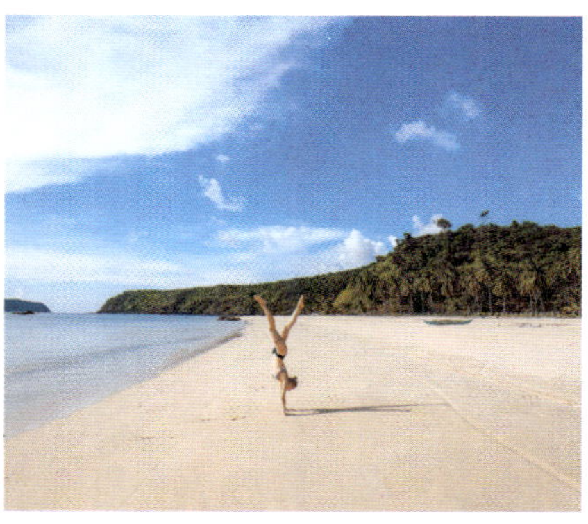

▲ *Taking selfies in remote locations can be challenging. Place your camera or smartphone on a solid surface, ideally using a tripod. There are compact and lightweight travel options, such as Gorillapods.*

Toa Heftiba
@heftiba.co.uk

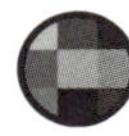

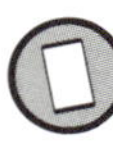

TECHNIQUE

When: The best times of the day for light tend to be at dawn and dusk.

Where: If you're in a well-visited location, try looking for a new view that you haven't seen photographed by anyone before.

How: Look for lines and forms that will act as focal points for your image.

Filters: Lark desaturates reds and intensifies blues and greens to add punch.

TAGS

#sunset #photopills (app developers love a nod)

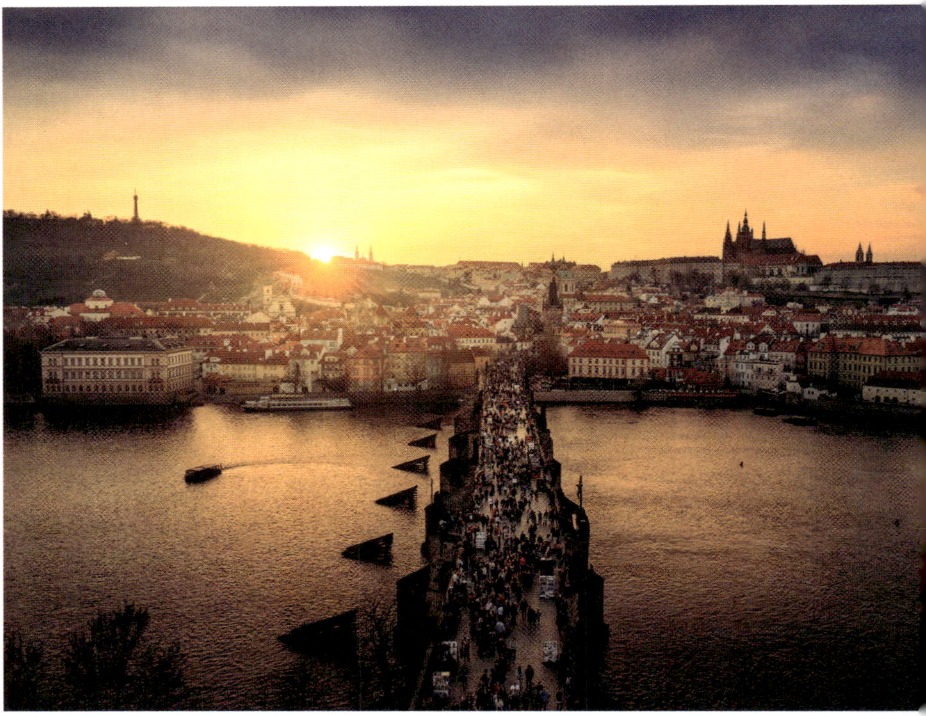

TIME YOUR VISIT

As noted elsewhere, a lot of good photography is about the light, so for this assignment you will be setting out to photograph an attractive location in the best possible light. The light that appears at sunrise and sunset has a certain cast, especially during the times known as the "golden hours," because of the warm light. The precise timing of the golden hours depends on your latitude on the world map, and on the time of the year.

Getting the timing right is essentially about maps and math, and there are apps that can help you plan your shots before you even visit a location. Perhaps the best known is PhotoPills, which has features to help you calculate where the sun will rise and set at any location, enabling you to be in just the right spot at the right time. It will even show you what to expect by using augmented reality.

It is worth thinking about other factors as well. For instance, clouds can help you because they create a more diffuse light that eliminates harsh shadows. Try capturing a single location in different lights and creating a Best Nine (see Assignment 26).

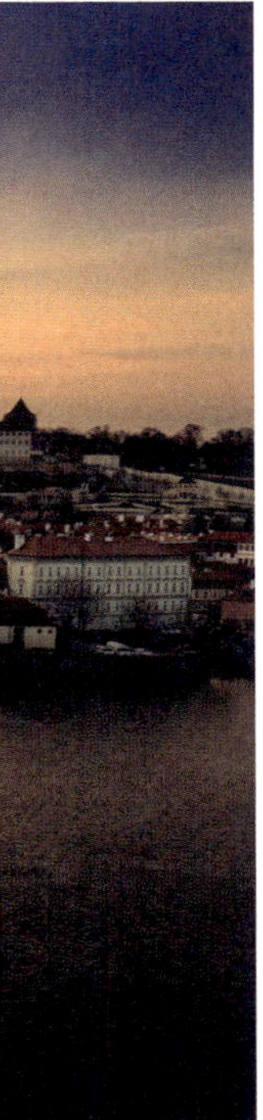

◀ *Picked up by the makers of the @photopills app, this shot of Prague was made easy for Vilim Hlušicka by the app telling him when and where the sun would set.*

Vilim Hlušicka
@hlushoot

TIP

Spend time with PhotoPills so you can grasp the relative motion of the sun and moon. Make sure you've set the date for the day you plan to shoot and tap the augmented reality (AR) mode—a line on the screen will show you where the sun will set.

ASSIGNMENT JOURNAL

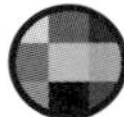

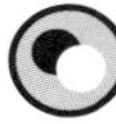

TECHNIQUE

When: Shallow depth of field works well with portrait photography or for capturing details of objects.

Where: Indoors for portraits and shots of objects; outdoors for flowers and insects.

How: If you're using a camera, select an aperture size of f/2–f/5.6, and be careful to keep the subject in focus (a tripod may help). On a smartphone, turn on Portrait mode if it is available.

Filters: Boost the Saturation and Contrast, or try converting to black and white, but avoid Sharpening tools.

TAGS

#dof #depth #photography

IN AT THE SHALLOW END

Using a shallow depth of field means that only your subject—or even a small part of your subject—stands out in crisp focus while anything nearer to the lens or further away is out of focus. Shallow depth of field is created when a camera's lens has a relatively wide aperture (see page 10). The aperture is measured in f-stops, which are fractions, so f/1 is a much wider aperture than f/16. On a digital SLR, select Aperture Priority mode and open the aperture as wide as you can.

Shallow depth of field has long been a tool in the photographers' armory, particularly for portraits, where traditionally it required a large camera and lens. Now, smartphone photographers have the tools at their disposal to achieve similar effects and, if applied carefully, these can look just as magical. For this assignment, shoot images using a shallow depth of field, or try using the Portrait setting on you smartphone (this goes by different names depending on the make of smartphone—Apple call it Portrait Mode, for instance). Be aware that the results on smartphones can be mixed, depending on the quality of the software and the data available. Post and tag the most striking image you achieve.

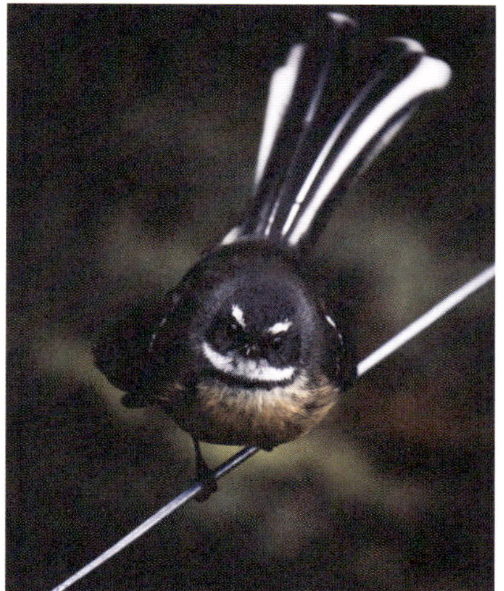

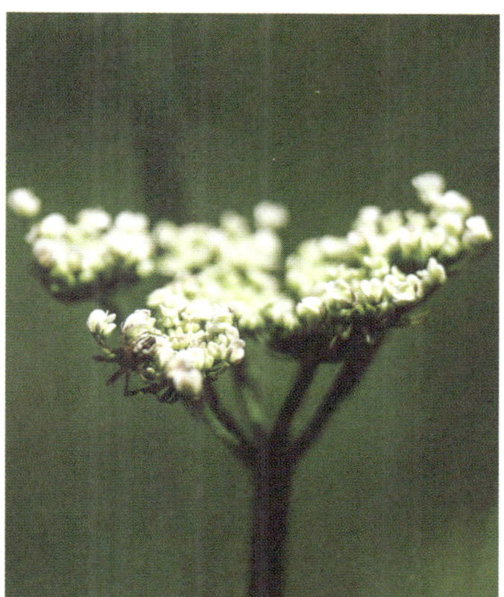

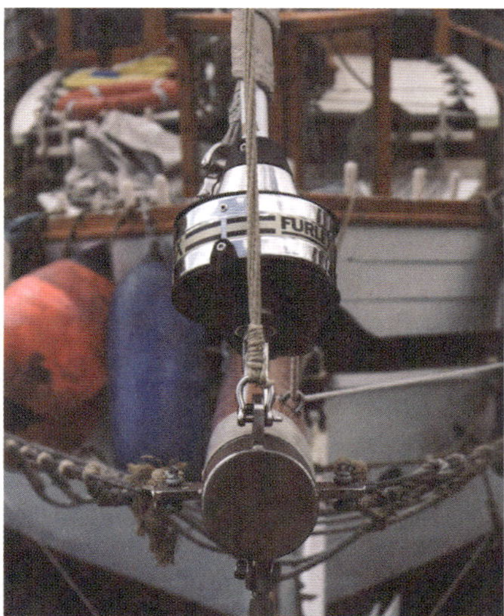

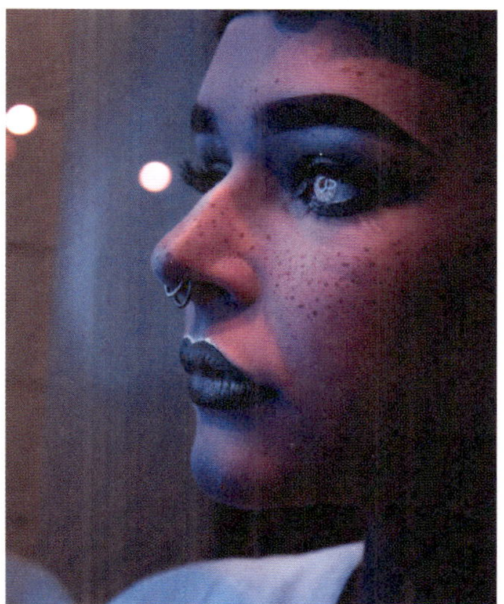

▲ *Belgian outdoor photographer Yoal Desurmont took these photographs with a focus on depth. The shallow depth of field means we see just the detail the photographer wanted to show, but almost nothing of the surroundings except their general tone—perfect for this kind of shot.*

Yoal Desurmont
@yoal_des

TIP

If you're using a phone's shallow focus effect, try to shoot in good light; the better the original photo, the easier it is for the phone's AI to identify a subject (usually a face) and digitally blur the other areas.

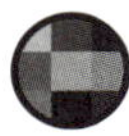
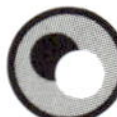
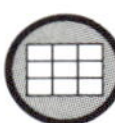

TECHNIQUE

When: Opportunities for selfies, portraits, and model shots, day or night.

Where: Any location, but you need sufficient light—natural light is best.

How: Pay attention to how light falls on the face—especially the eyes—and experiment with different poses.

Filters: Match your intent, but radial filters like Hudson and Sutro work well.

TAGS

#eyes #killerlook #portraitperfection #portraitoftheday #instaportrait

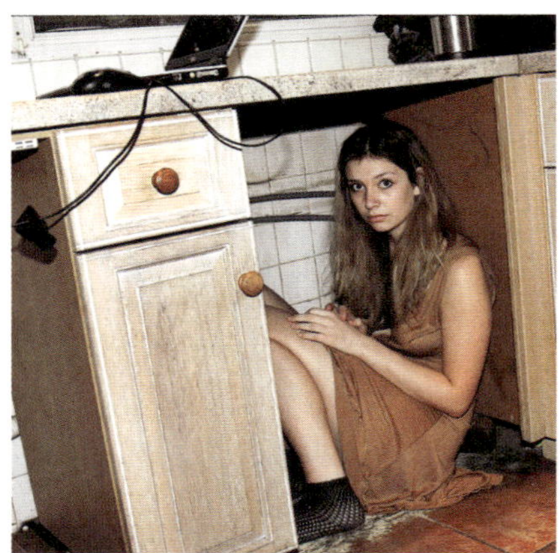

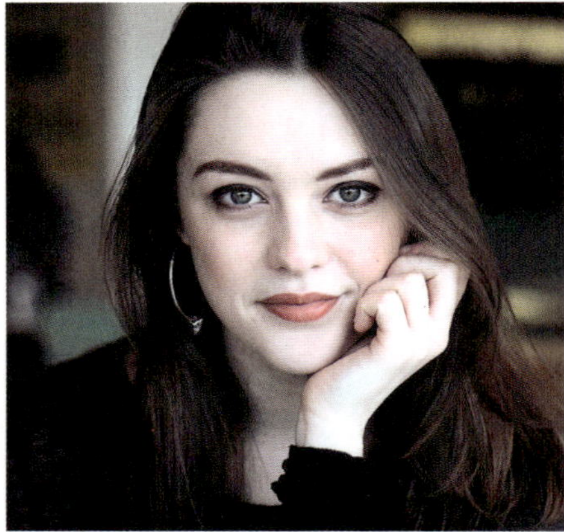

▲ *Mark Wilkinson is the photographer behind the hit YouTube channel Weekly Imogen. The portrait on the left has a lot to take in, but the angle means the subject looks up at the lens, revealing the white around three sides of her pupils. In the close-up portrait on the right, the addition of gentle "catchlights," or reflections, from a window behind the camera makes the eyes, and the look, even more striking.*

Mark Wilkinson
@unexpected.tales

THE LOOK

Models have a certain way of looking into the lens that works every time. Why? Because we're genetically programmed to look at the eyes first. Professional photographers obsess about getting the eyes just right, but your phone is already pretty smart—the camera app will look for faces and eyes and make sure they're in focus (unless you tell it not to). This means that you can spend your time directing your model to give you the right look.

Instagram is populated by millions of photographs of people, and this assignment is all about capturing a compelling portrait that stands out from the crowd. There are a few simple tricks of the trade. First, try not to get people to pose in a formal fashion, as it will make them stiffen up. Instead, encourage them to relax and ask them to look at the lens—chat with them for a short while, and take a few photos in natural pauses to give you a selection. Second, to display the eyes, and to get a more flattering look in general, ask your subject to push out their chin and tip their head down a little. This has the added bonus of helping you to avoid pointing the lens up your subject's nostrils. Third, when your model is standing, don't have them face you straight on—get them to turn their body sideways and then turn their head toward you.

Finally, try to be mindful of where the light falling on the eyes comes from. A nice, square window behind the photographer will create a shape reflected in the eyes that adds an extra dimension to a close-up, and at a distance you'll still get a sparkle. With these tips in mind, create a portfolio of Instagram portraits of one model that has a consistent "look."

TIP

It's important in posed portraits to get the eyes right every time, not just in focus but positioned in a prominent part of the frame, and conveying a meaningful look or emotion.

ASSIGNMENT JOURNAL

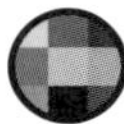
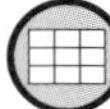

TECHNIQUE

When: In soft lighting, such as natural light through a window, which helps viewers to "read" a subject's expression.

How: Something as simple as where the hand falls on the face can make all the difference between looking as though you're thoughtful or on the verge of tears, so experiment.

Filter: No Filter, but consider adding a touch of Contrast.

TAGS

Emotional tags are among those with the biggest appeal, but keep it simple: #happy #love #sad

INSTA EMOTION

Part of Instagram's appeal is that it is a highly successful way to convey a human message. With photography front and center, Instagram crosses demographics more easily than other forms of social media, and also connects people around the world. And what could be a more human way to communicate than with emotion?

Emotions are popular tags, but conveying a feeling photographically—beyond simply letting the face do it for you—requires a bit of thought. For this assignment, set out to grab a reaction shot. Use a prop such as a letter, to which you or your subject can react, and capture the emotion of that moment.

A nice advantage of this approach is that you're visually encouraging the idea of emotional engagement. This, in turn, helps to promote "engagement" with your post—increasing replies in the comments section—and this will cause Instagram to promote your image, resulting in more Followers and Likes.

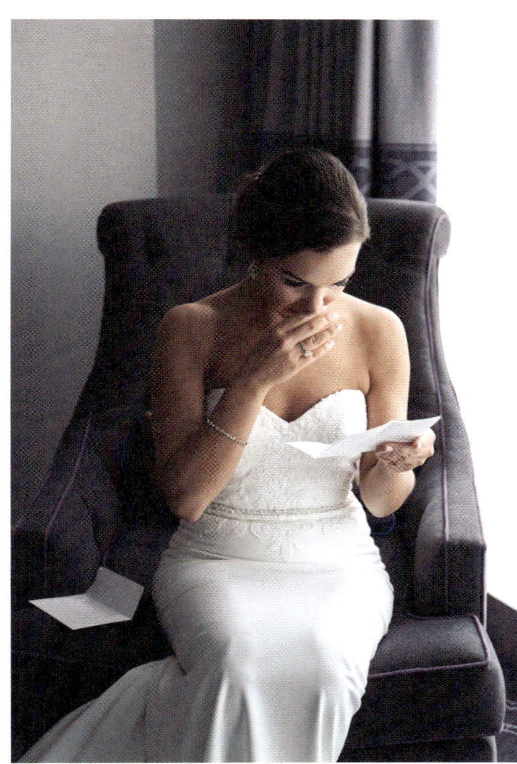

◀▼ *This is a classic reaction shot by wedding and boudoir photographer Critsey Rowe. She takes advantage of Instagram's sequence tool to add a close-up of the paper, just to emphasize the story behind the emotion.*

Critsey Rowe
@critseyrowe

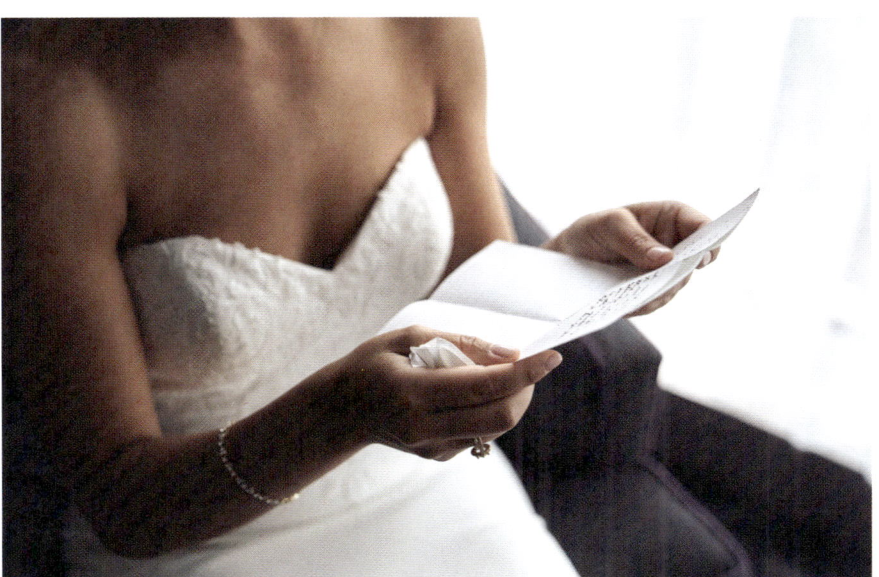

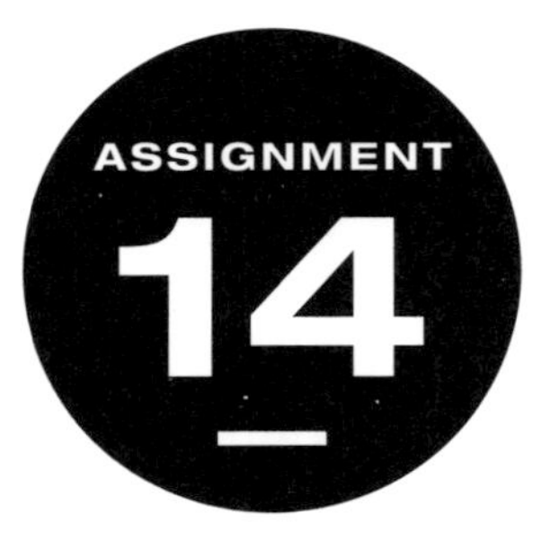

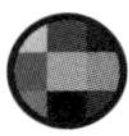

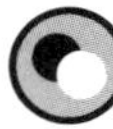

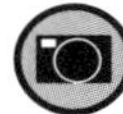

TECHNIQUE

When: When the camera is completely still.

Where: Where there is movement you can blur, such as flowing traffic or water.

How: With an ND filter over the camera lens or using your smartphone's smart brain.

Filters: Rich, contrast-enhancing filters such as Juno and Clarendon.

TAGS

#longexposure #ndfilter

LONG EXPOSURE

Since the days of film, photographers have wowed viewers with long exposures. The idea is simple: if the camera's shutter is open long enough, then anything that moves during the exposure will blur, while anything that doesn't move remains solid. This can be used to create car-light trails in low light, or surreal flat and misty water.

On a digital camera, neutral density (ND) filters can be used to achieve long exposures, by reducing the amount of light entering the lens and reaching the digital sensor, forcing the camera to open the aperture more and/or for longer. Smartphones can achieve a similar effect by shooting a series of photos, one after the other, and then analyzing them. Any shake from your hand will be eliminated as the software automatically lines up the images and then performs various effects, including simulating long exposures.

Many smartphones are capable of long exposures; on iOS, enable Live Photo mode and swipe up to see the Long Exposure option while you're viewing the image in Photos. However, if your Android phone doesn't have this feature, look for the Long Exposure Camera 2 in the app store.

Your assignment is straightforward: create a long exposure that brings light trails or blurred water to your Feed.

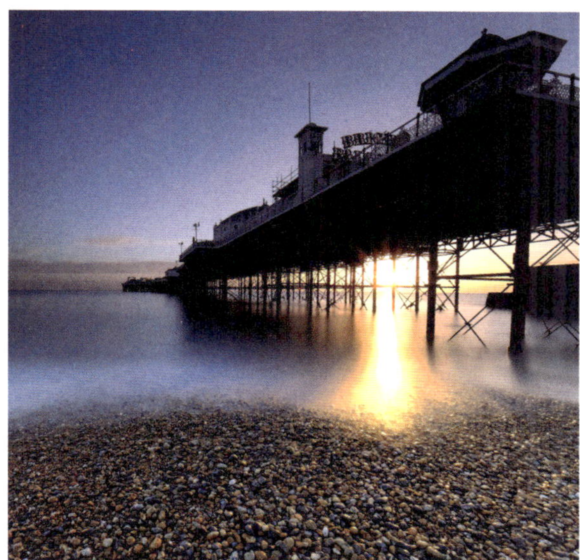

Gordon Laing
@cameralabs

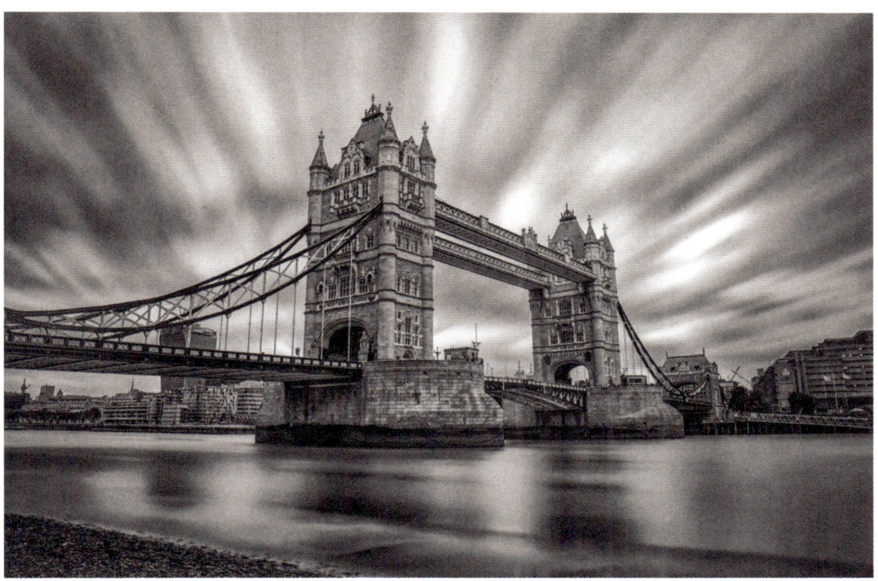

▲ Attaching an especially dark ND filter will force a camera to compensate by keeping the shutter open long enough for objects to move and water to blur, as Antony Zacharias has done here. It is vital the camera doesn't move, so a tripod is essential.

Antony Zacharias
@antonyzphoto

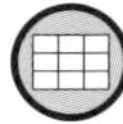

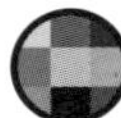

TECHNIQUE

When: Daytime, within moments of the food being cooked (especially for food like eggs).

Where: Near a window for natural light.

Filter: It's best not to use any filter at all, just adjust Contrast—discoloring food makes it appear unpalatable.

TAGS

#food #foodie #cheeseontoast #greenchutney #thingsontoast #lunchtime #cheeselovers

#FOODIE 1: DRESSING

Food photography underpins many successful blogs and supports more than one publishing house, where successful cookbooks depend on everything looking mouthwatering and perfect. The same demands are now being made on Instagram, where there is a profusion of foodie photographs celebrating a chef's creation or a diner's delight. Many of these show great food, without being great photographs, and some simple techniques can make your images far more appetizing.

Capturing the right look is all about preparation and set-dressing. So, for this assignment you will give some thought to the meal you're photographing—and its colors—and work back from there. Pick your tableware carefully, looking for complementary colors (see Assignment 03), or use simple white tableware if that is impossible. You might also choose to use attractive ingredients to dress the scene. Finally, don't forget the significance of positioning cutlery—use it to create leading lines, directing the eye around the image, from one plate to another (if there are several plates), or just into the frame. Then, shoot before the light changes!

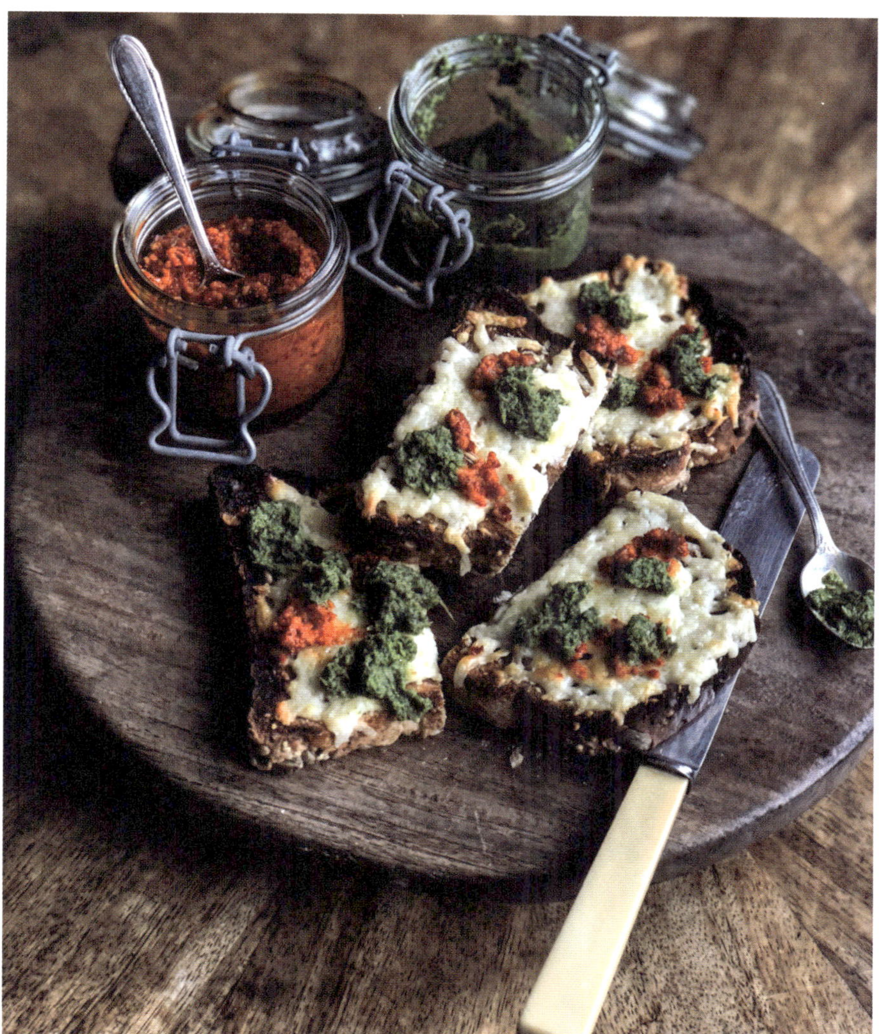

Matt Inwood
@matt_inwood

ASSIGNMENT JOURNAL

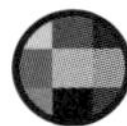

TECHNIQUE

When: Planning is needed to capture your food at its best, just after cooking.

Where: At home. This assignment takes food photography to the next level, so best not to attempt it in a restaurant!

How: Search your home for surfaces with interesting textures that you can use to create artistic backgrounds.

Filter: Best avoided! It's important to keep the food looking natural—stronger greens and blues will make food appear inedible! But try increasing Brightness and Structure, and reducing Contrast a little.

TAGS

#food #foodie #foodporn #foodgasm

#FOODIE 2: BACKGROUNDS

As you develop your food photography, you will find that developing your own style is the way to create a feeding frenzy around your Instagram Feed. One important step toward this is the realization that it is not just all about the food. Backgrounds can be just as important in creating your own foodie personality. A well-chosen backdrop can be the difference between a shot that leaps out and grabs you, and one that your viewers swipe straight down your Feed. Your assignment brief is to create some great images of food by concentrating on creating some great backgrounds.

Look at contemporary food photography in cookery magazines for inspiration—you'll find all kinds of exotic surfaces beneath and behind plates. Cookbook photography in particular has seen a shift from the binary, clean linen or homely looks of decades past toward all sorts of industrial, grungy, and shabby-chic backdrops. Anything goes, really, and a wide range of surfaces will serve you well to give your food posts that extra special something. There are more ideas on the following pages.

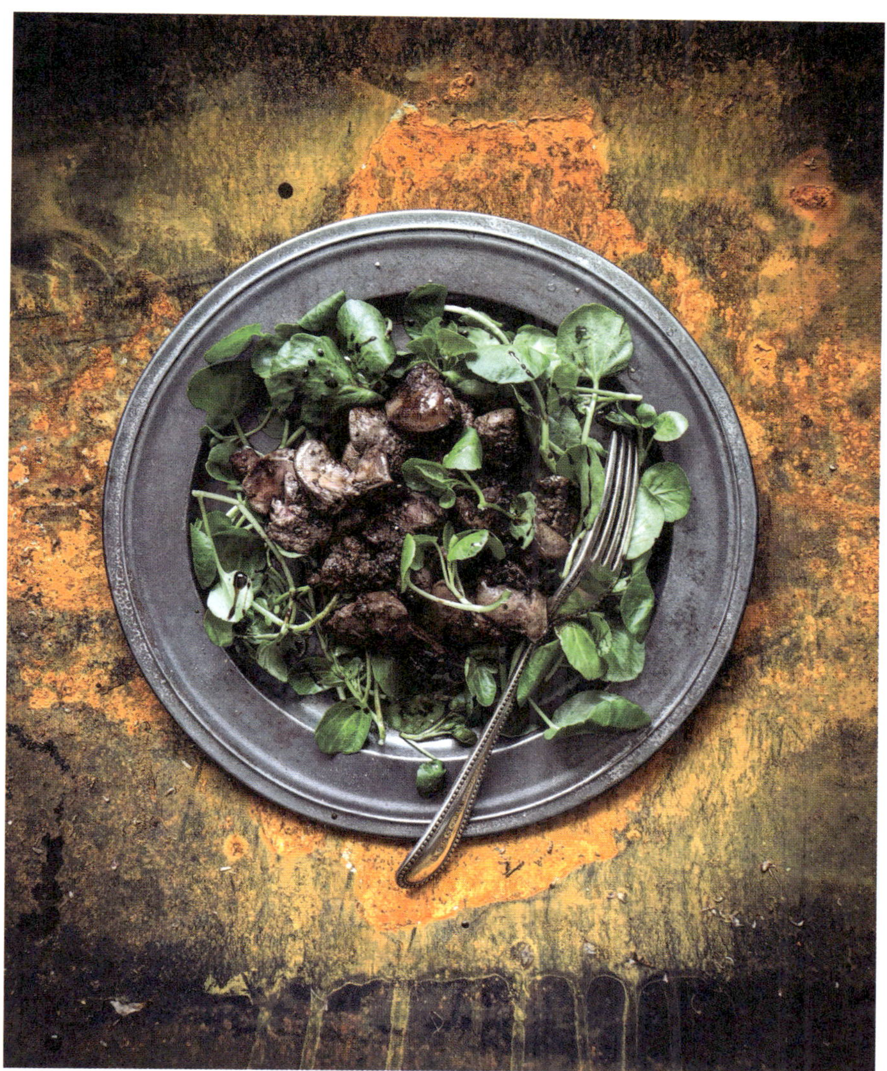

ASSIGNMENT JOURNAL

▲ *A rusted piece of sheet iron forms the most striking of backdrops to this simple (iron-rich!) chicken liver salad.*

Matt Inwood
@matt_inwood

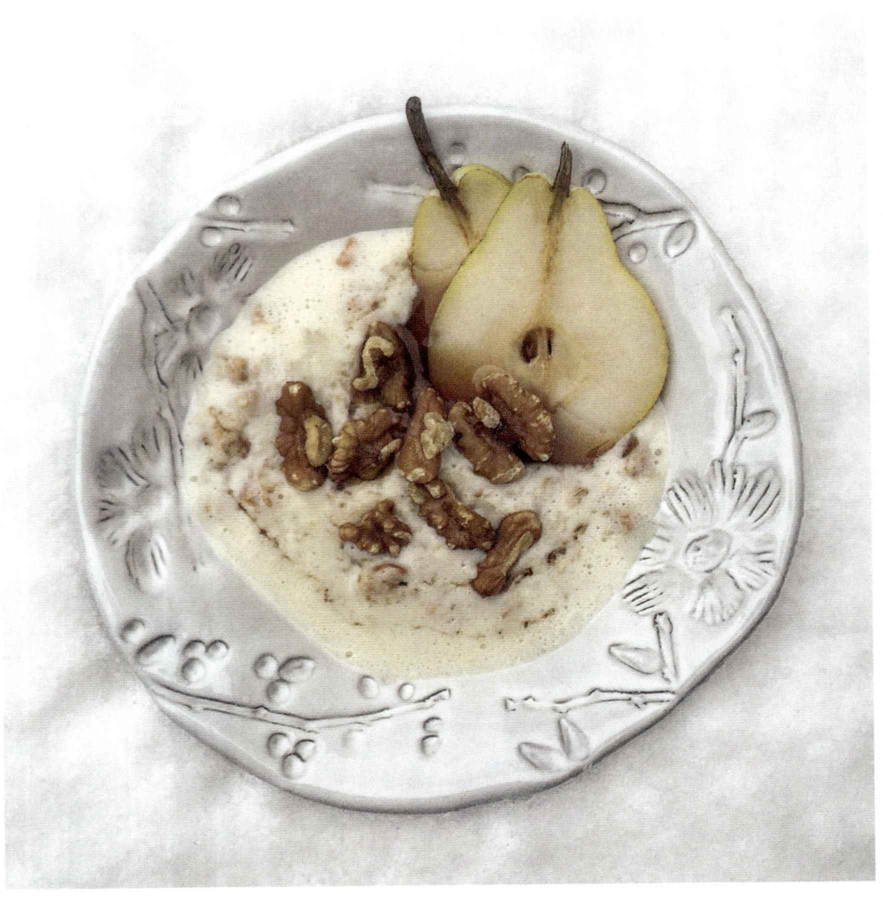

Go for plain backgrounds with enough surface texture to provide interest, but not so much heavy detail or pattern as to detract from the food. Beware of high contrast, such as white plates on dark backgrounds or dark plates on white backgrounds. If the light is less than ideal, then too much contrast between the plate and the background can prove difficult for a smartphone camera to cope with.

Keep thinking about light in every aspect of what you photograph and how you set up your shot. Remember that surfaces play a key part in the lighting and color balancing of your shots. Dark surfaces will absorb light and bright surfaces will reflect it. A midtone gray is a great neutral ground to put food on—it's no surprise you see so much metal and slate in food photography these days. Wood (especially worn wood) is always a good surface—it suggests comfort, homeliness, and a completely accessible style of cooking.

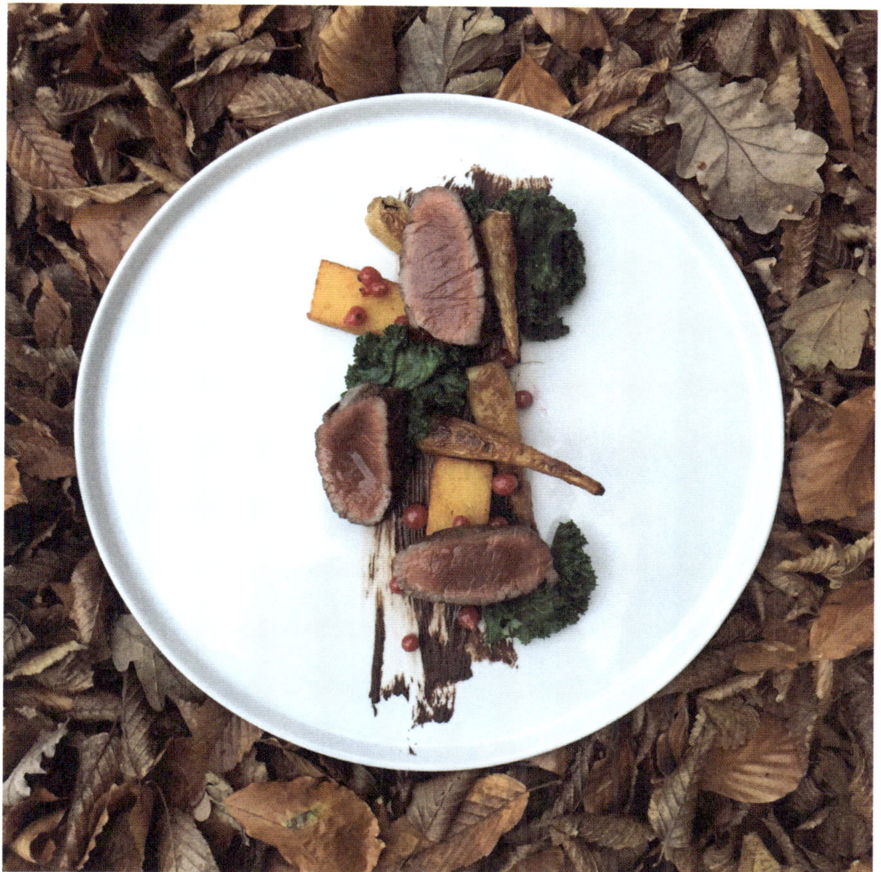

TIPS

- Interesting surfaces and textures are all around you. Look at the floors, inside and outside. Try turning over tables, where you might discover that the unvarnished reverse is more attractive than the lacquered top.

- Collect surfaces of all sorts of materials and look for peeling paint, rust, and decay. They can present wonderful and highly unusual textures and colors.

- Hold on to unusual packaging or foreign newspapers—you never know when they might be useful in your food photography.

TECHNIQUE

When: Shoot in good light.

How: Tap on the type to ensure it's in focus.

Filter: Make sure you use the Sharpness filter. Experiment until you're happy that the type is crisp but not aggressively artificial-looking.

TAGS

Choose tags that reflect the type of content: #inspiring (for quotes); #lyric (for song lyrics); #happy (always a good one to sneak in, as it's a perennial high-scorer).

WORDS MATTER

During our formative years, we start to recognize the faces that are important to us, but very soon—while we still have "brain plasticity"—we're introduced to words and their importance. This is significant because it means that, just as we instinctively look at people's eyes, we also automatically look closely at type. The sharp, contrasting shapes draw us in, even when they're very small.

That's why, despite the fact that Instagram is a pictorial medium, people still pay attention to words—and that means it's a good idea to make them the focus of your shot. This also explains the arrival of Type mode for Stories in Instagram. For many, Stories *is* Instagram, and it allows you to type over photos or video, or simply type onto a colored background for each post. Since Stories flash up briefly you can use the text to tell a narrative that people can page through.

You can find Instagrammable words in all sorts of places: neon signs, tattoos, street signs, graffiti, and protest placards are all rich sources. To complete this assignment, set out to photograph something that includes words people can connect with—for example, a neon sign that can be read as an inspiring message or a piece of advice.

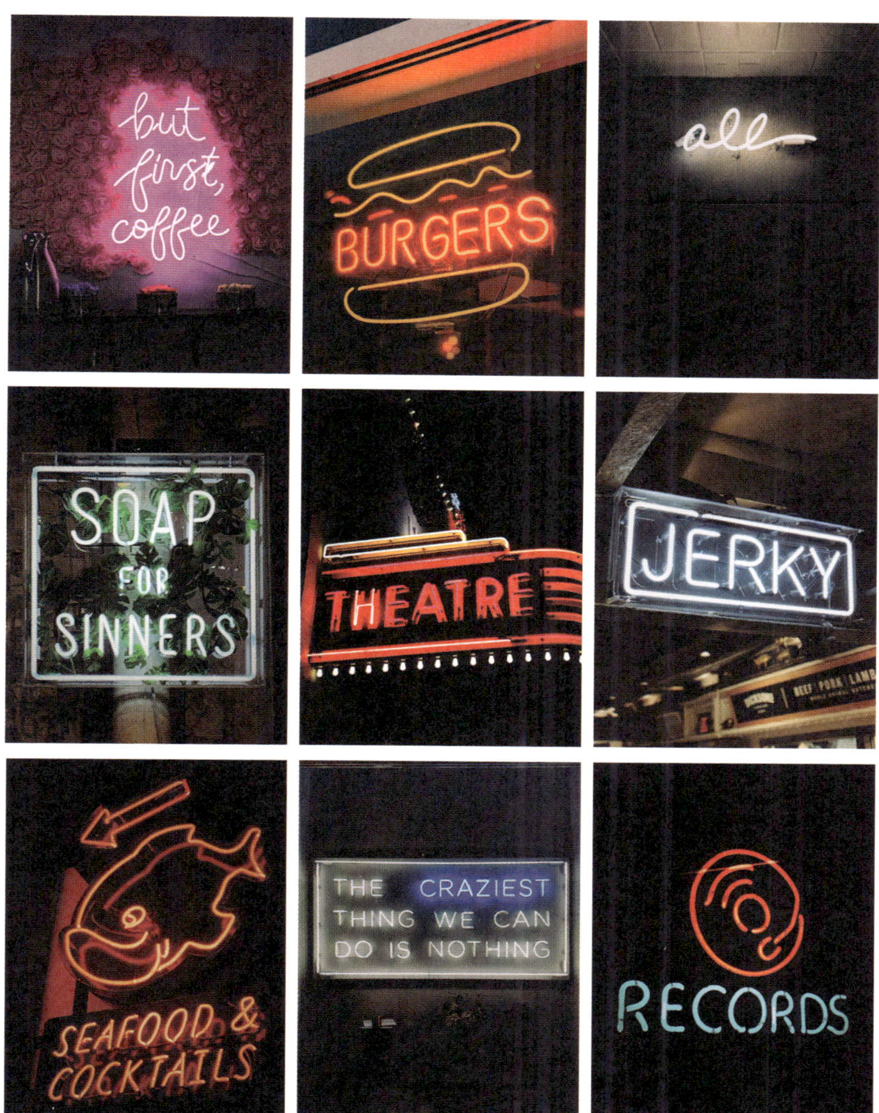

▲ *If one word in glorious neon can be eye-catching, a whole collection of neon signs can create a powerful Instagram identity. You can use photographs of a distinctive style of sign to draw attention to particular words and directions, or simply to create a piece of street-inspired collage art.*

Jon Tyson
@jontyson

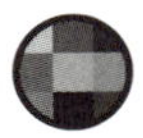
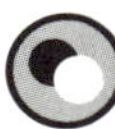

TECHNIQUE

Where: From the Eiffel Tower to the Sydney Opera House, the world is not short of iconic locations.

When: If you can, aim for good or interesting light.

How: Look for an unusual viewpoint, or try varying the height or angle of your camera or smartphone.

Filters: Charmes adds contrast to make city locations seem more vibrant.

TAGS

#(Use the place name) #(Use the city name)

SEE IT DIFFERENTLY

Even the hippest traveler targeting unique and undiscovered locations will chance upon a tourist hotspot from time to time. And most of us seek them out. Instagrammers frequently post shots of iconic locations captured in the same way, from the same viewpoint. So, for this assignment, when you next find yourself at beauty spot, make it your business to find a different view from all the others you see online.

One approach is to vary the height from which you take your photo— too many tourists shoot at eye-level, a legacy of eyepiece viewfinders on older cameras and people's reluctance to duck. A smartphone gives you the flexibility to compose from ground level or from above the crowd, so take advantage of it.

A key feature of great photography that is often forgotten is the quality of the light, and how it falls on your subject. Day or night, think about how the quality of the light, and the highlights and shadows, affects your composition. The good thing about Instagram is that you can also choose a Filter to match—converting a shot to black and white, for instance, often makes harsh shadows look stylish.

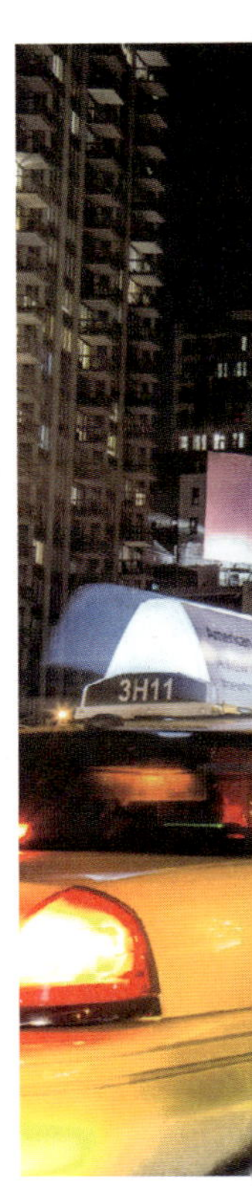

▼ *As a professional travel photographer, Deborah Sandidge makes money from her images by finding new, appealing angles on popular destinations. This shot of the famous Flatiron Building—arguably the world's first skyscraper—was achieved by using a tripod set below the tops of the cars, right in the road junction, and using a long exposure. If you are attempting this on a smartphone, you might need an extra app, such as Slow Shutter Cam.*

Deborah Sandidge
@debsandidge

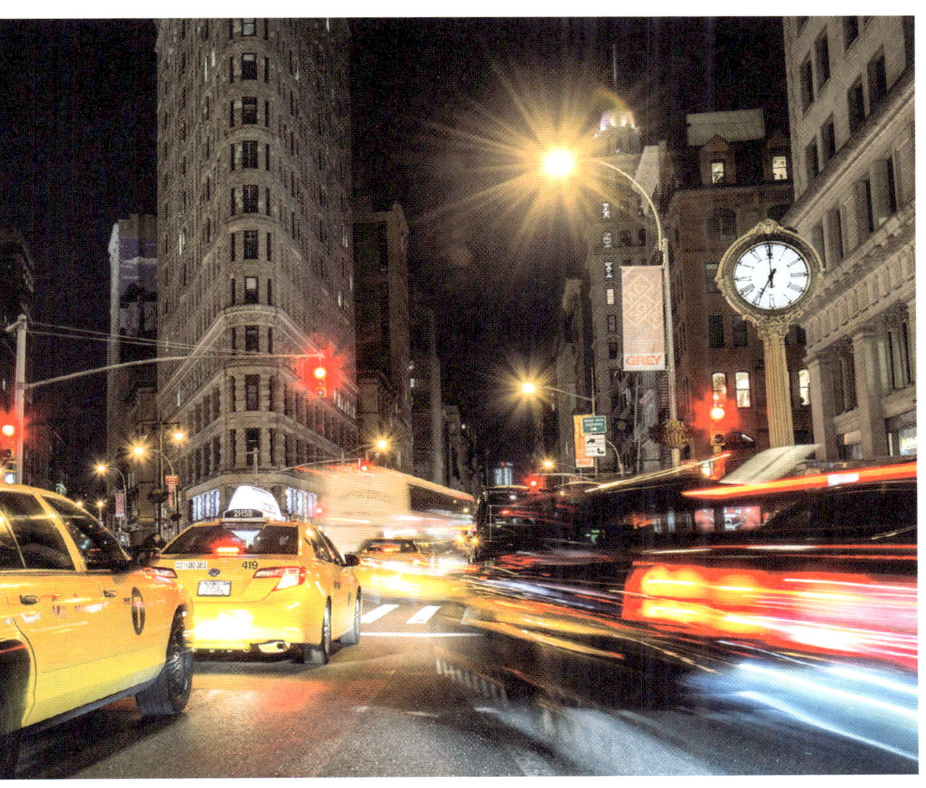

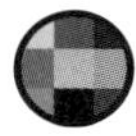

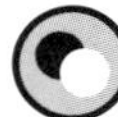

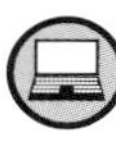

TECHNIQUE

When: On a clear night.

Where: In rural areas, away from the light pollution from urban streetlights.

How: Position the telescope on a tripod and choose your subject. Carefully line up your smartphone's camera in the center of the telescope's eyepiece, then take the shot.

Filters: Boost Contrast and Saturation using the Edit tools or use a Filter like Clarendon.

TAGS

#moon #lunar #astrophotography #photohacks

THE MOON ON A STICK

Photographers are inclined to get a little bit obsessed with optics. They can start to think that there is no problem that cannot be solved by adding another lens—for the price of a house payment—to the kit bag. In practice, though, Instagram doesn't really reward the extra investment. Most people are viewing on a mobile device screen and—despite very high resolutions—they aren't able to perceive the level of detail that such technology delivers.

You can take advantage of this by doing things that are little impromptu. For this assignment, try holding your smartphone camera up to a telescope's eyepiece to grab a photo that would exercise even a practiced astrophotographer. If you're likely to do this frequently, there are products available to help you mount a smartphone on an optical device and line up the camera more easily.

As you start looking up at the heavens in this way, you'll discover a whole world of Instagrammable images: from the extraordinary surface of the Moon to the shape of the Milky Way. This technique can also be applied to other subjects: for example, by placing your smartphone on the lens of a bird-spotting scope.

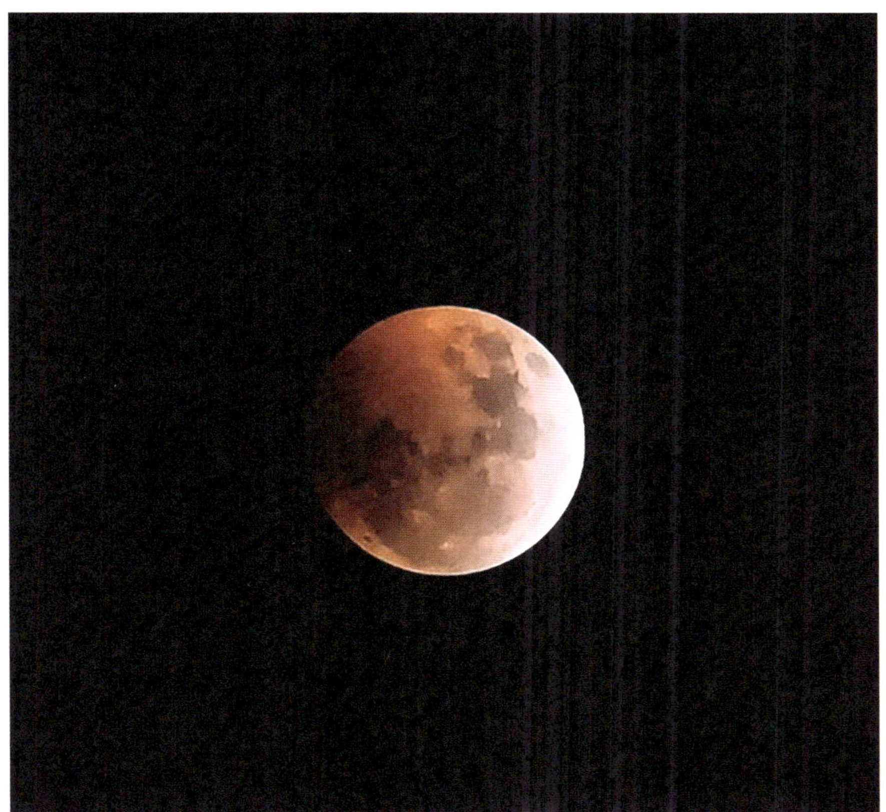

▲ *Daring drone racer Jonathon Davis found time to capture this blood Moon during a solar eclipse. It was cropped slightly within Instagram. Shooting with a phone and a telescope might not create a print-quality shot, but it can capture an image that has huge impact when viewed on a phone screen.*

Jonathon Davis
@skitzofpv

ASSIGNMENT JOURNAL

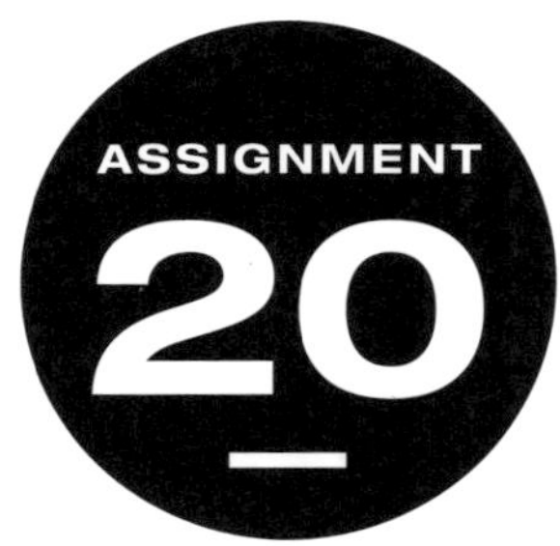

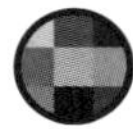
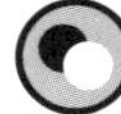
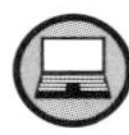

TECHNIQUE

When: Early morning offers crisp air and sharp lighting angles.

Where: Public squares and flat spaces—make use of beaches and walls.

How: Look for interesting shadows in bright light—it helps if the shadows are of recognizable subjects. Wait for people to move into shot to create intriguing interactions between shadows.

Filters: High-contrast (Mayfair, X-Pro II) or black and white (Inkwell).

TAGS

#blackandwhite #bnw #shadow #silhouette #blackandwhitephotography #lightandshadow

SHADOW CRAFT

Although the presence and quality of light are crucial in photography, the absence of light can also play its part. Shadow areas can be just as impactful, and—in the right light—all the world is your shadow puppet theater. For this assignment, your mission brief is to exploit the drama of shadows in your photographs.

Good shadows are easy to "read" for the viewer if they appear on plain surfaces, such as a flat beach, or a simple repeating pattern such as a brick wall. With those cast on the ground, try to get the shadow to point somewhere interesting. For sharper shadow edges you will need a single distant light source (such as the sun, at 93 million miles away!). Focused artificial light from a projector is a good backup when experimenting indoors. Playing with shadows is also great for your hashtags, since you can use the ever-popular black-and-white filters and corresponding tags.

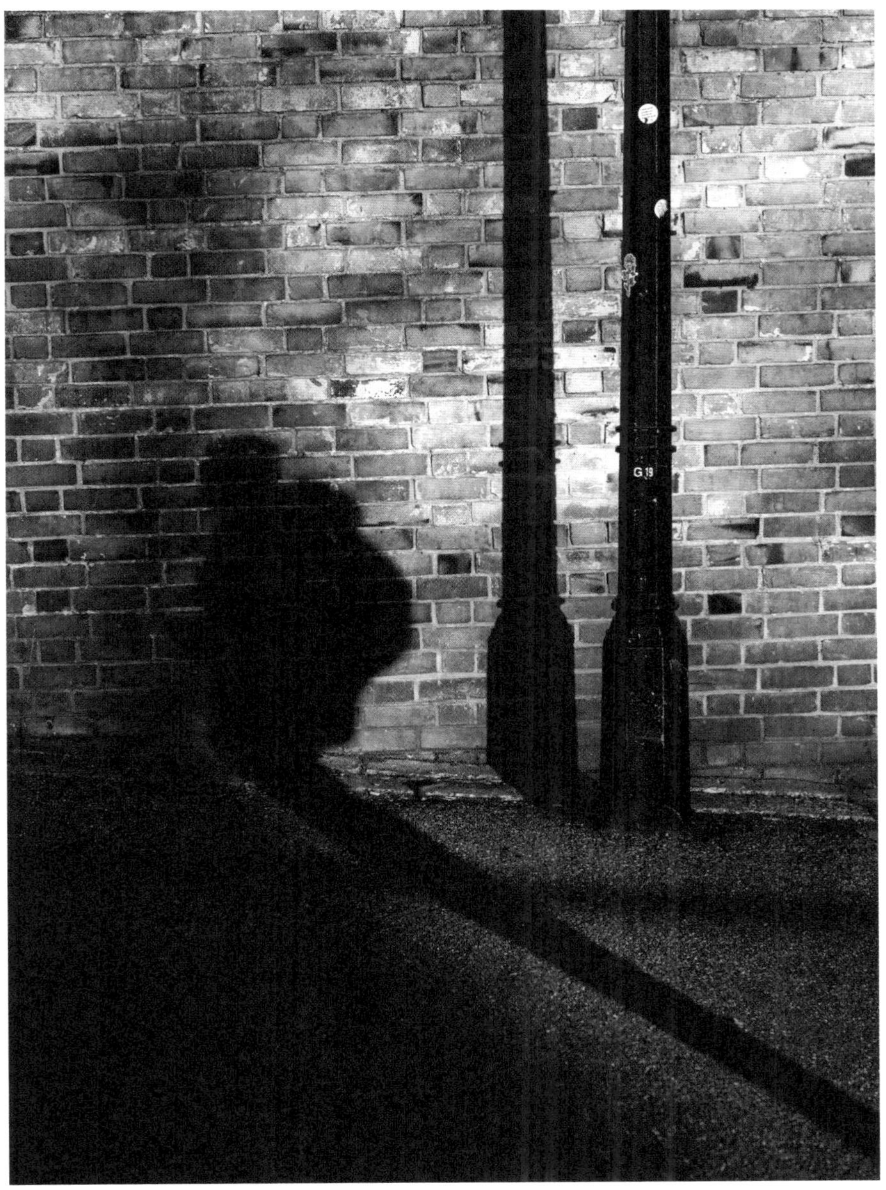

▲ *Winter light casts shadows on the wall. For a sharp, angular look, stand further away and use a telephoto lens if you have one.*

Sean Tucker
@seantuck

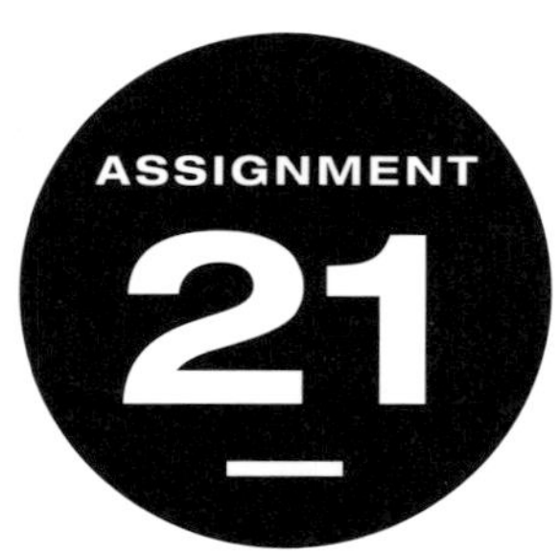

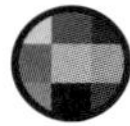
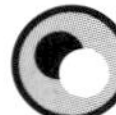
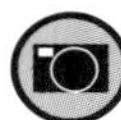
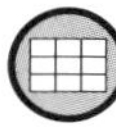

TECHNIQUE

When: Any shot of a landscape during daytime.

Where: In any large or interesting landscape.

How: Shoot someone (it can be a selfie using a self-timer) against the backdrop or object. Your "for scale" person should be far enough into shot that you can see all of them.

Filter: Ideally pick one that favors the scene. Boosting the contrast with a filter such as Dogpatch will likely help your subject stand out and emphasize the scale.

TAGS

#scale #ice #walk #explore

SCALE THE HEIGHTS

When you share your best shot of an awesome place on Instagram, you know the scale of what you're seeing... but your viewers might not. For this assignment, your brief is to capture the scale and drama of an exotic landscape or location by placing someone in the picture. This will allow anyone viewing the photograph on your Feed to immediately get a sense of scale.

To avoid the photograph becoming about the person—their main purpose is, after all, purely functional—it's a good idea to encourage them to either be walking away from the camera or admiring the real subject. You can also make them more abstract, perhaps by capturing them in silhouette.

Ideally, your helper should also be dressed appropriately (if the man in the example here was wearing swimming trunks it would be a different shot entirely). If you can't find anyone to appear in the image, and you're somewhere safe, use your camera's self-timer and photograph yourself.

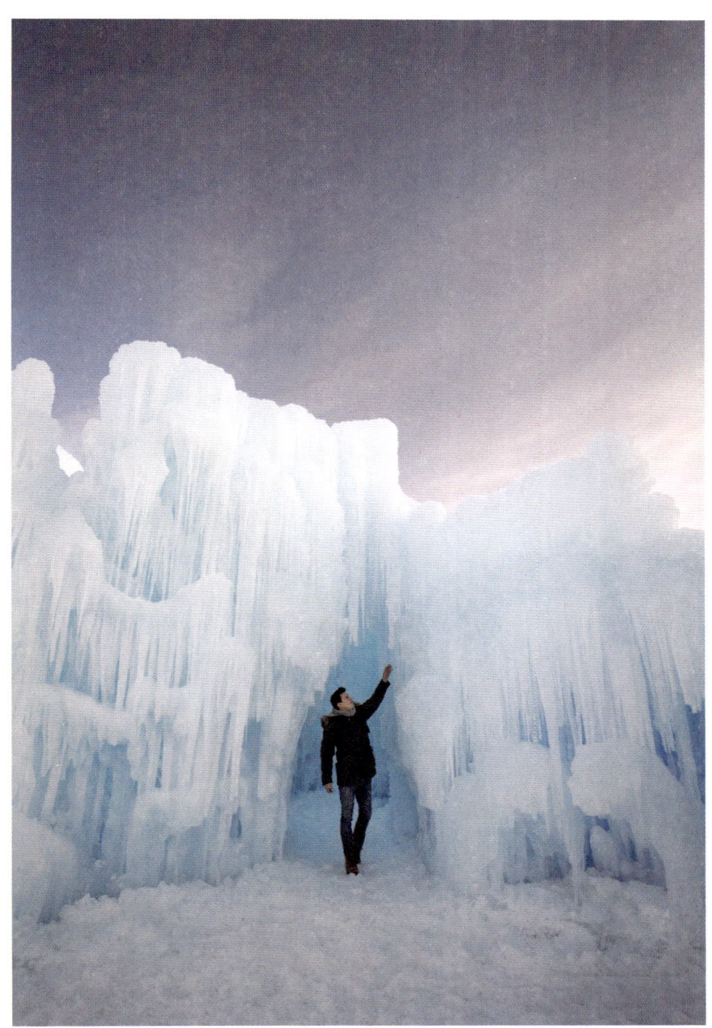

▲ *This view of the Midway Ice Castles (@icecastles_) was captured by globetrotting photographer Kirsten Alana. Without @dante.vincent in shot to give a sense of scale, the ice formation might just be the one that grows in your ice box when you don't clear it out.*

Kirsten Alana
@kirstenalana

TIP

When you're using a figure to give an image context, the shot shouldn't be about their clothes or their face. You can also clear up ambiguous scale in pictures of small items (from products to model railways) with recognizable objects such as a coin.

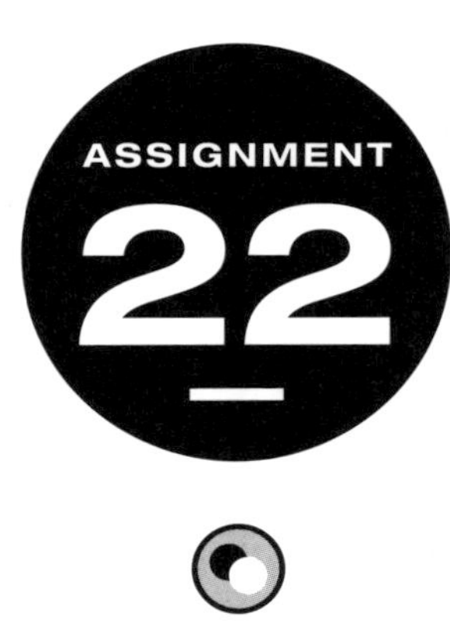

TECHNIQUE

How: To create a story, swipe your finger right from the main page of the Instagram app. A new screen will appear with a swipeable menu at the bottom. Normal allows you to pick an image or video from your Feed, while Create lets you work on a plain background.

Filters: You can swipe left and right over the main image to change the Filter, but try the Superzoom effects too (these are essentially video filters).

TAGS

Use the location tag Sticker and tag any co-stars in your selfies. The Stickers system won't allow you to use more than one of each type, so you can't go overboard!

TELL A STORY

These days, Instagram is not only about photographs, or even video clips. For many people, Stories is their main interaction with the app. Stories began as an immediate function, in which posts self-destruct after 24 hours, an approach most likely inspired by the popular SnapChat app. Now, two things really set Stories apart. First, Instagram is very good at drawing your followers' attention to your posts during their short life. Secondly, mastering Stories is not so much about the image or video, but how you augment it with effects, text, and stickers.

Once you have invoked the Stories feature and chosen your background (a photo, video, or newly-shot clip), it's time to add stickers. Tap the Sticker icon and start to experiment. You can also use Instagram's AI, so that a sticker follows an object in your video as the object (or the camera) moves. Just tap and hold for the "pin" option. Your assignment is to master the Stories feature and use it to introduce your Followers to your photographs or video in an entirely new way.

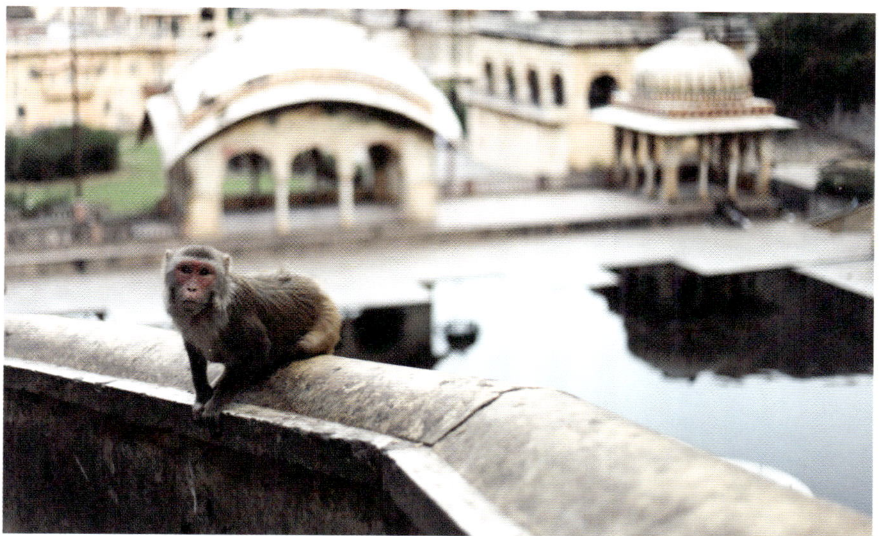

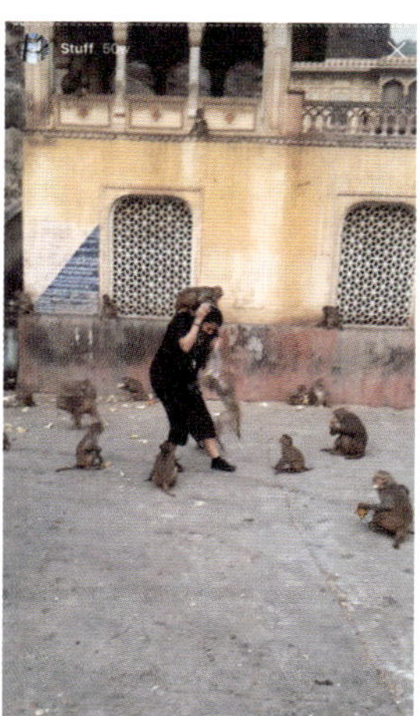

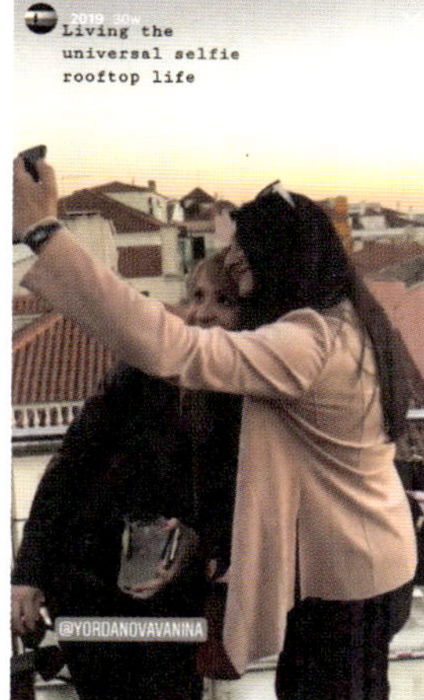

▲ *Street photographer Tanya Nagar uses Stories to share some behind-the-scenes moments from her photography (the video clips of monkey-infested Jaipur give an idea what it was like to capture the still), and a good bit more of her personality.*

Tanya Nagar
@tanyanagarphotography

TIP

It's always better to shoot photos and videos in your main camera app, but for Stories, shooting in the Instagram app allows access to a range of effects. Swipe the shutter button right to see different whole-screen video filters. Once you've got one you like, tap the shutter for a still image or hold for a clip.

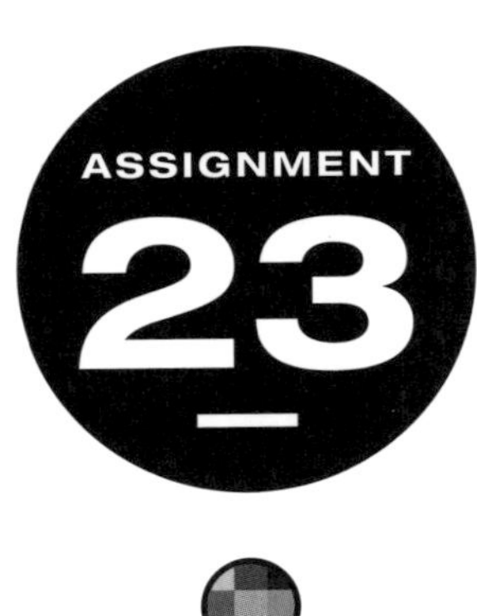

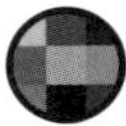

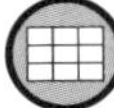

TECHNIQUE

When: Overcast, midday light to avoid reflections; early morning light for harsh shadows; early evening for blue sky with lights; night for lights in windows.

Where: Look for the modern quarters of cities, often in business or cultural centers, where contemporary architecture provides sharp lines and interesting reflections and textures.

How: Think about what the architect was trying to achieve.

Filters: Inkwell and Walden Vespa work well.

TAGS

#architecture #architecturephotography

#ARCHITECTURE

Urban environments afford great opportunities for creative photography. For this assignment, your brief is to use architecture to build your Instagram following. Find a corner of a town or city that you find visually interesting. Pay attention to the interplay of lines and surfaces, and look for abstract images of walls, windows, and other architectural features. Be precise with the buildings' lines and make sure they are perfectly composed in the frame. Use your feet to explore every angle, while taking advantage of all the perspectives your camera offers—wideangle lenses (x1 or x0.5 zoom on a smartphone) are traditionally popular with architectural photographers.

Professional architecture photographers sometimes use tilt-shift lenses (which avoid lens distortion and ensure vertical lines). You can't do this with a normal lens or smartphone camera, but try to get the lens as vertically parallel with your building as possible. Use the Grid overlay on your smartphone or camera to help you line up shots carefully, and correct any distortions using perspective correction software. Curate a set of images that complement each other or follow a theme, and then post your best nine photographs and see what feedback you receive.

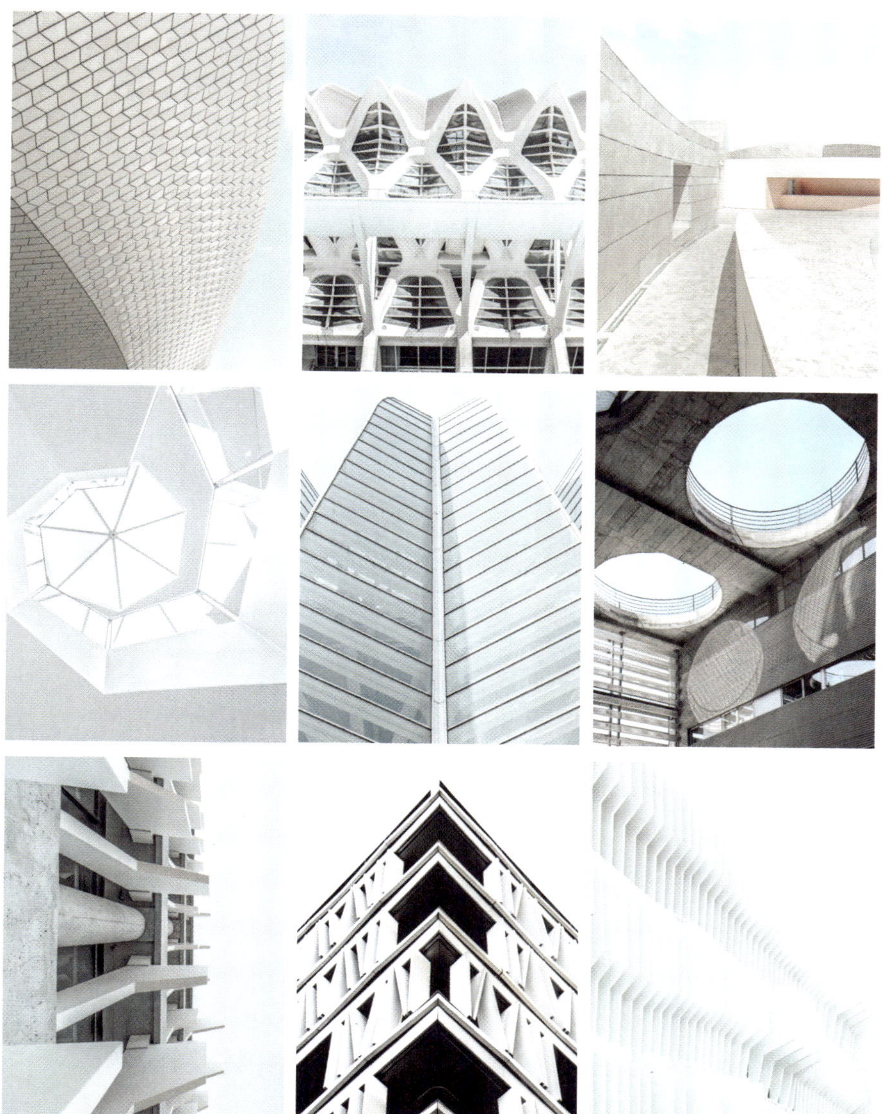

▲ *The architectural photographer here makes use of his designer training, looking for leading lines and using perspective tools in Photoshop or Instagram to force at least one of the lines to be perfectly straight.*

Joel Filipe
@joelfilip

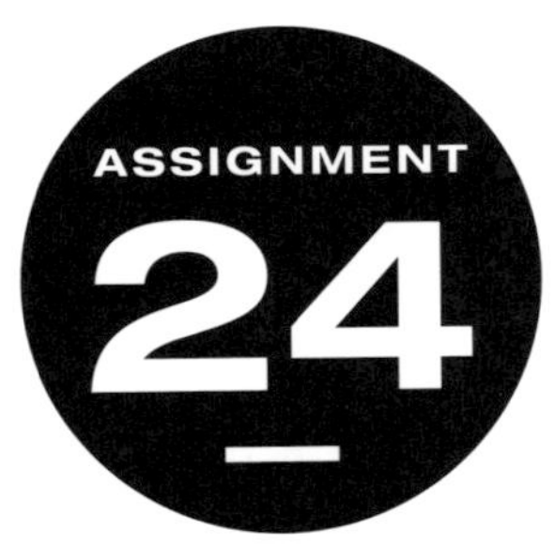

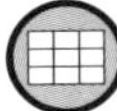

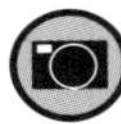

TECHNIQUE

When: Aim for soft light (for instance, under an overcast sky) so your shadow doesn't become a problem.

Where: Wherever you find street art.

How: Street art on its own can be interesting, especially if it's colorful and detailed, but try adding to it by posing in front of it, or shooting from an unusual angle.

Filter: Increase the Contrast of your image.

TAGS

#(location) #(artist) #wings #selfie #angel/demon

▶ *Whether you are photographing a pet, a portrait, or a selfie, street art like angel wings can provide a themed studio backdrop for your Feed.*

BEYOND THE SELFIE

"Bad artists copy, great artists steal," as a great artist once said, and there is plenty of material on the streets for the sharp-eyed photographer to "steal" and turn into some Instagram art of their own. Your assignment here requires you to do some leg work, by heading to a city, walking the streets, and photographing your take on some original street art. There is a huge variety of street artists' work all around you, including spectacular masterpieces that can be creatively photographed and adopted to add to the personality of your Feed.

A classic example is "angel wings," which you can often find painted on a wall, although just how angelic they are depends on the subject—fallen angels don't always discard their wings. If you see them, you'll know where to stand. It's a good lesson in creating interesting portraits by interacting with impactful backgrounds, which can work with street art, graffiti, or even interesting gaps in architecture (negative space). Don't forget to tag the artist's name if you know it.

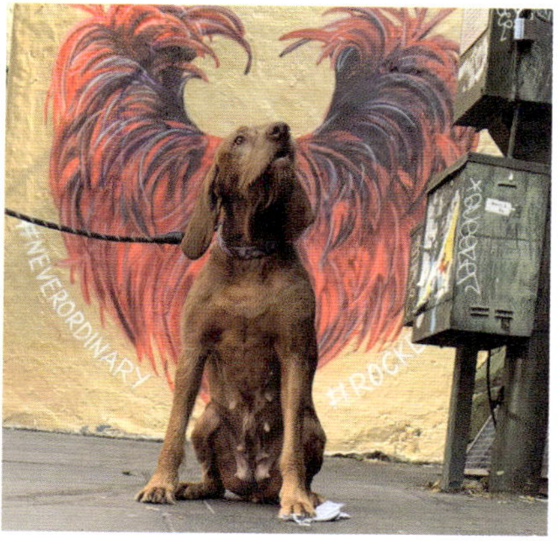

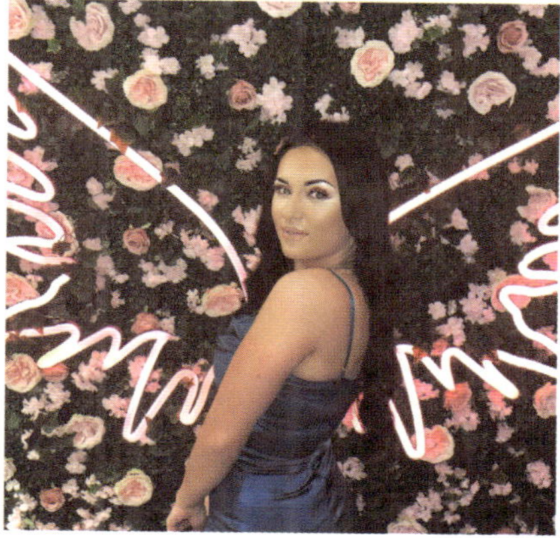

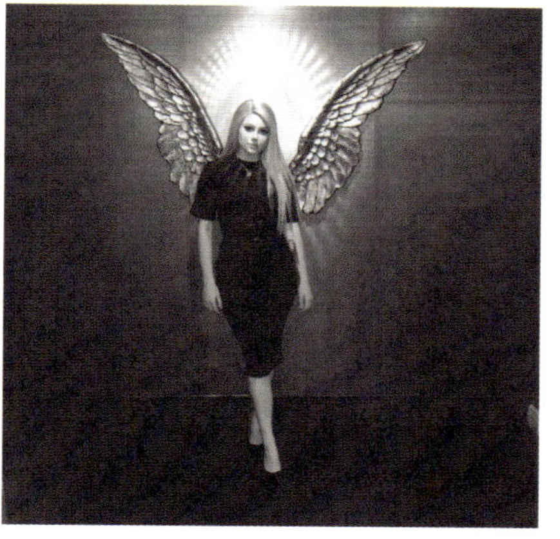

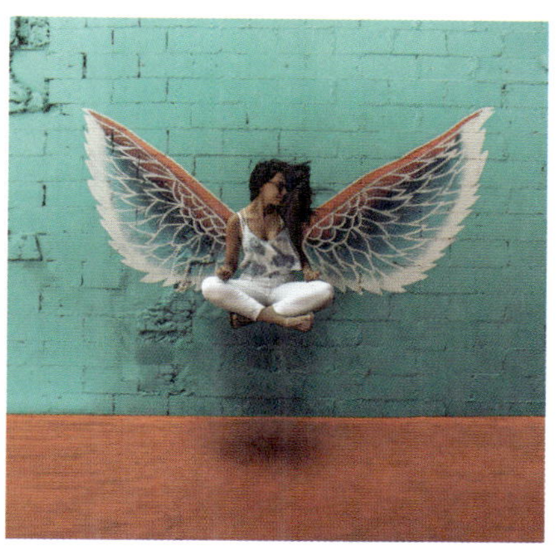

▲ *From top left, clockwise:*

@finnstagram_vizsla

@shannrosetiger

@designecologist

@bethmizuki

ASSIGNMENT JOURNAL

TIP

You might be surprised that most photos tagged as #selfie are clearly not shot with the camera (or even a stick) in hand, so there's nothing to stop you using that tag for shots where you ask a friend to compose and take the shot.

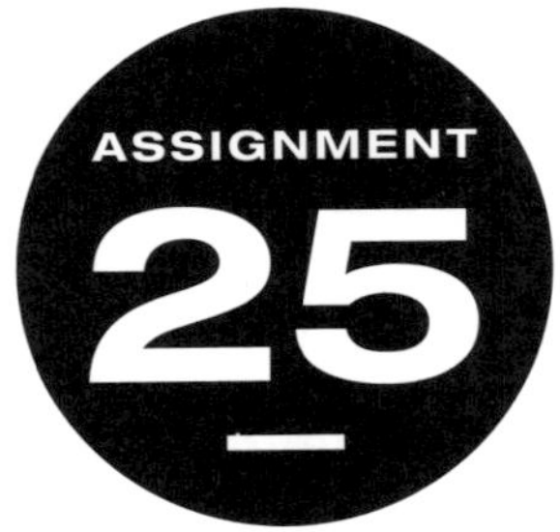

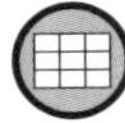
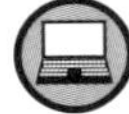
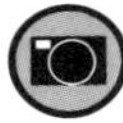

TECHNIQUE

When: Shooting around midday prevents long shadows obscuring too much ground detail.

Where: Aim to hover your drone over safe, neutral locations.

How: If you don't have access to a drone, look for high viewpoints that enable you to shoot directly down—but stay safe!

Filters: Although Instagram filters might not be needed, a real, physical neutral density (ND) filter over your drone camera is useful on sunny days.

TAGS

#drone #dronestagram #aerial #dji

ASSIGNMENT JOURNAL

► *Founder of Unequal Scenes and African Drone, Johnny Miller uses the aerial view to emphasize the disparity in living conditions in South Africa and around the world.*

Johnny Miller
@johnny_miller_
photography

GOD VIEW

This assignment is all about finding a new perspective, and shooting images from overhead. Raising your lens directly above the subject provides a completely different approach to telling a story, and gives your Instagram followers a whole new angle on things. Even on a small scale, this approach can create interesting results—taking a bird's-eye view of a plate, for example, offers a more impactful composition than a menu-style side view.

If you can lay your hands on a drone, then you can raise this assignment up among the gods. Modern drones offer some very Instagram-friendly tricks, such as quick, animated sequences that start with a hovering selfie and then appear to leave you in your very own tiny planet. These sequences are achieved by flying back and up very fast, while keeping the camera trained on you, followed by a certain amount of automatic image processing.

Drones are great at providing compellingly different views of the world. Fly your drone up to 300 feet (100m) and point the camera straight down to reveal more detail of your environment than most mapping services, while still feeling "real" to the viewer.

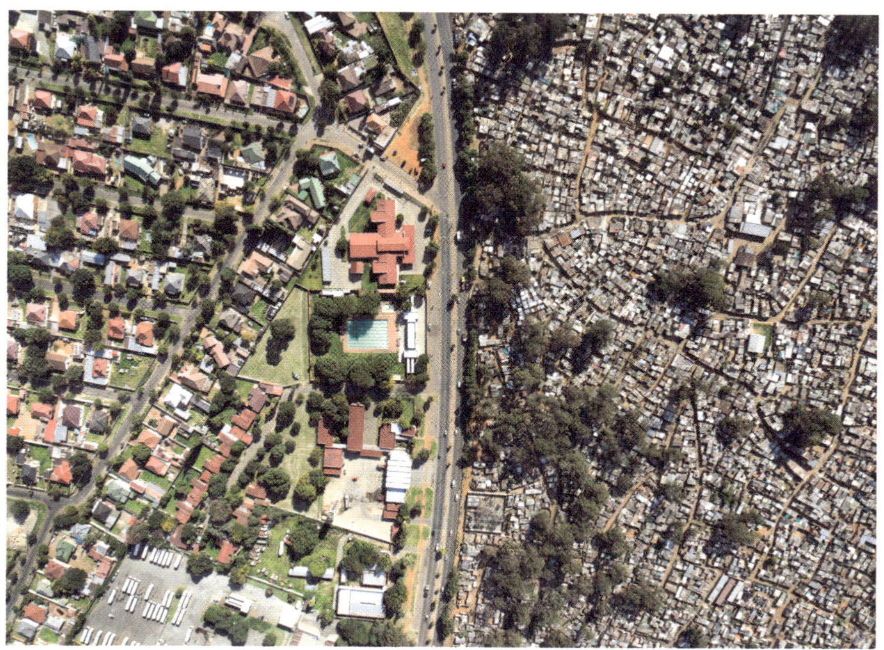

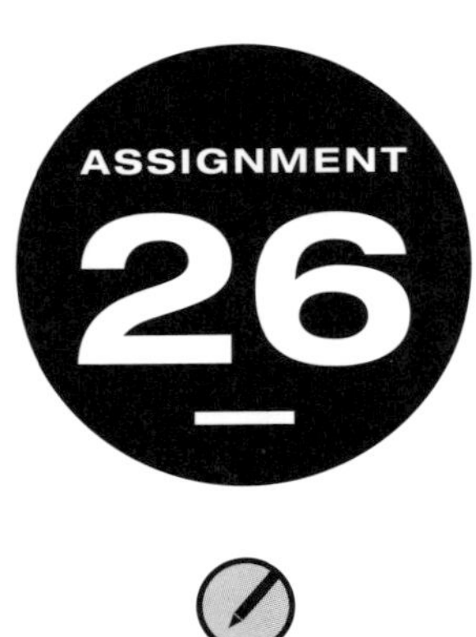

TECHNIQUE

When: At the turn of the year.

Where: Via the website 2017bestnine.com.

How: Enter your Instagram ID at 2017bestnine.com and wait for the result. Post the result using the buttons at the bottom of the window.

TAGS

#bestnine #bestnine(year)

▶ *The 3x3 grid looks good with most photos, but Marina Sersale also has a consistent style that makes for a really effective Best Nine.*

Marina Sersale
@eauditalie

BEST NINE

When a year turns around on the calendar, it's always worth having a little look back to review your photography. A nice way to share and celebrate past successes is by creating a Best Nine—this produces a three-by-three grid of your top images of the year, rather like a mini-Feed that can then fit into your main Feed. And that's what this assignment is all about.

You can find some assistance with this brief at 2017bestnine.com. (Oddly, the developers haven't snapped up bestnine.com yet, but you'll find that "2016bestnine" and "2018bestnine" both send you to the same place.) On the website, you'll see a search window into which you type your own handle. All you need to do is wait while a computer at the other end looks back through your most recent full year, identifies the most liked posts, and creates a new grid image which you can choose to share on your Feed. It will even generate the hashtag for you.

If you're doing this right at the beginning of the year, be prepared for a small wait—the website's server gets a bit busy then. It's also worth a look through other people's Best Nine using the #bestnine(year) tag.

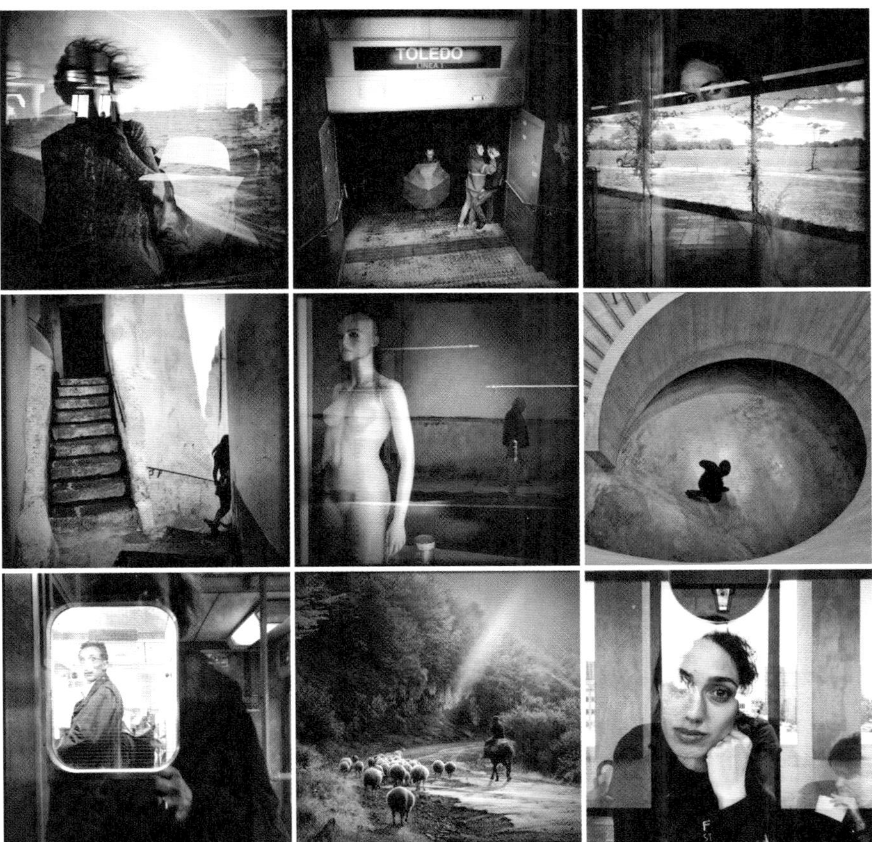

TIP

Another interesting angle on Instagram grids is splitting images across the grid so they look big in the Feed. Check out Pic Splitter or 9square apps.

ASSIGNMENT JOURNAL

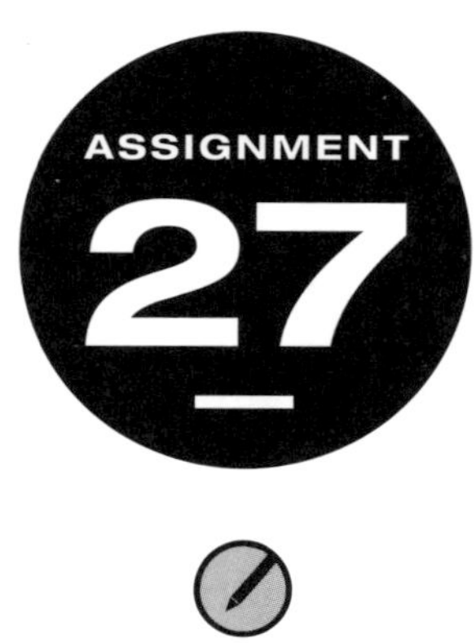

TECHNIQUE

When: Use Highlights when you want to collect some of your best Posts and Stories under different themed headings–this makes them easier for your Followers to access, too.

How: You will find that you have one Highlights circle in Instagram–to add a Highlight, tap on it and scroll back through your Stories entries. You can even find the ones that have disappeared from public view, to revive for Highlights. To create additional Highlights, press the circle with a plus icon and give the new Highlights channel a name.

TAGS

Be sure to add your location, as well as other hashtags as you would with your other posts.

HIGHLIGHTS

This assignment is all about mastering the Highlights feature in Instagram, which will help you curate your content to make it easily accessible to your Followers. If you decide you want to grow your account, you'll often be told you need to "have a brand"–I've said something similar in these pages. But this can be misinterpreted, with the result that your account ends up featuring similar pictures of similar-looking things. For the most part, this makes sense. The internet wants to label and pigeon-hole you, so co-operating with the process makes life easier for algorithms, potential Followers, and any public relations people who may be interested in what you have to offer. What if you do more than one thing, though, and don't want a separate account for each aspect of your life?

Thanks to Stories you can post pictures or video–featuring all the on-screen tags, GIFs, and other fun features–and save them into multiple Highlights channels which appear right at the top of your page. This means that they can be quickly located by visitors, allowing your viewers to access the aspect of your Instagram persona that most appeals to them.

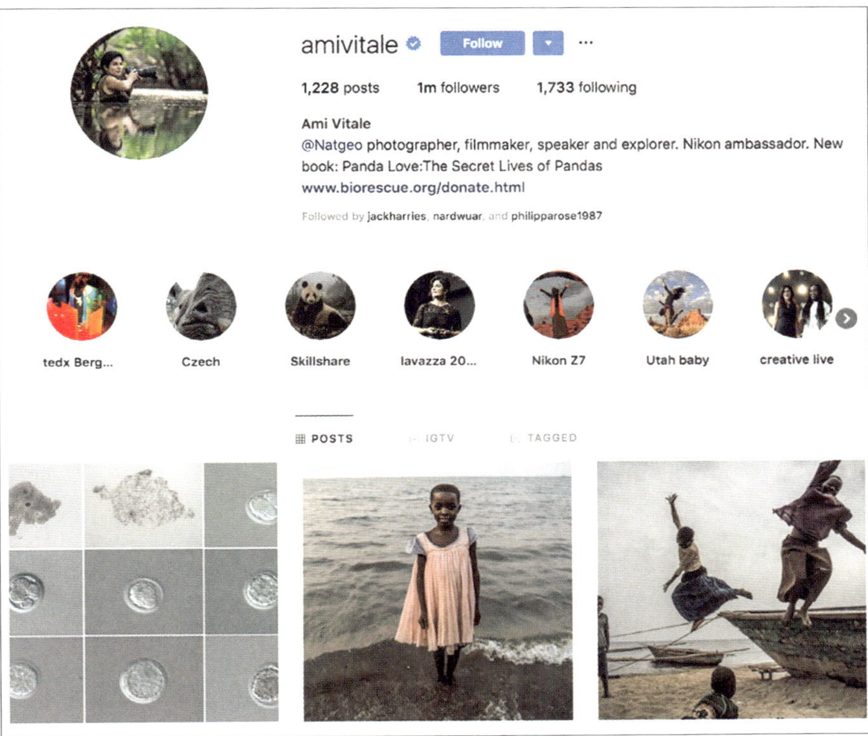

▲ *Ami Vitale has traveled the world, spoken on stage, photographed for* National Geographic *magazine, written a book, and shared her skills. By creating multiple Highlights folders, all of her activity is easily accessible without scrolling.*

Ami Vitale
@amivitale

TIP

Keep your Highlights channel name to about 12 characters if you don't want Instagram to truncate it. You can see that some of the categories here have been appended with "…" as they are over that limit.

ASSIGNMENT JOURNAL

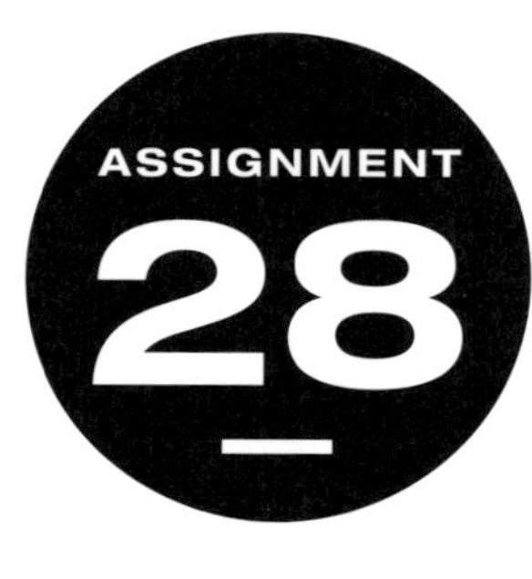

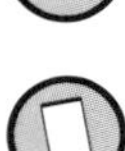

TECHNIQUE

When: Set aside time to experiment when you have a series of images you want to post.

Where: While taking a break in your favorite coffee shop.

How: Begin by downloading Planoly or Preview: Planner for Instagram. These apps will take you through the necessary steps. Avoid the paid-for features, especially if you're not working commercially. Simply import the image you want to work with and crop.

TAGS

It's best to add tags to each of the images in the series. The apps can provide hashtag recommendations, for a price.

PLAN YOUR POSTS

If you're an avid follower of one of the many beautifully curated accounts on Instagram that belong to creatives, you might wonder just how they manage to achieve such consistency on their Feed—even managing the impressive feat of spreading one picture across several squares with perfect joins. This doesn't come down to lining things up by hand. Written with marketers in mind, but useful for anyone who wants to curate the perfect Feed, there are a number of apps—such as Planoly—which allow you to upload pictures to a "preview" page to show how the pictures will look when you post them.

Using Planoly, you can drag posts into a different order and see the results before you actually upload them, and also schedule your post to appear at a time when more people are online. The app also helps you split a photo into multiple tiles that you can post. Your brief for this assignment is to download Planoly or Preview and try planning a week's posts, including splitting an image into a grid of nine tiles.

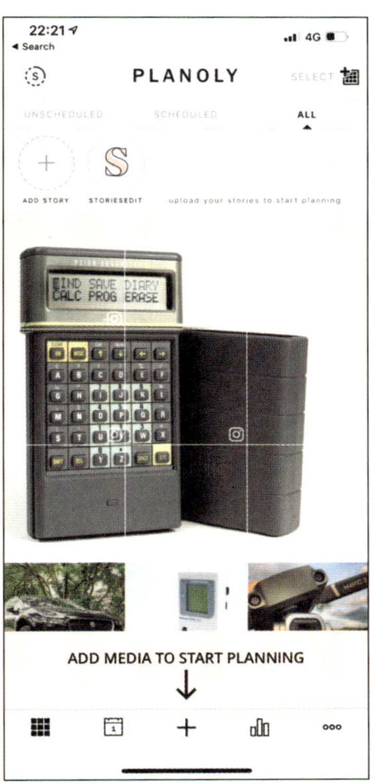

◀ *Here's Planoly in action. The app asks you to add your images, and you can edit them, move them around, and experiment with a variety of looks, previewing your posts as they will appear on your Feed.*

Tech Yearning
@tech.yearning

1 Choose your picture

Planoly is designed to follow the Instagram workflow, so the first step is to select a photo from your phone's catalog with the + button. Once you have selected your image, you will see a grid pattern icon. Use this to choose the tiles, or use the multiple image icon, depending on the arrangement you want to create.

2 Transfer to Instagram

In Premium mode you can use the app to upload all your tiles directly to Instagram, or you can save a few pennies by transferring the tiles yourself, one at a time.

TIP

If you're only interested in creating attractive grids with your posts, then you could opt for a less feature-rich app, such as 9square.

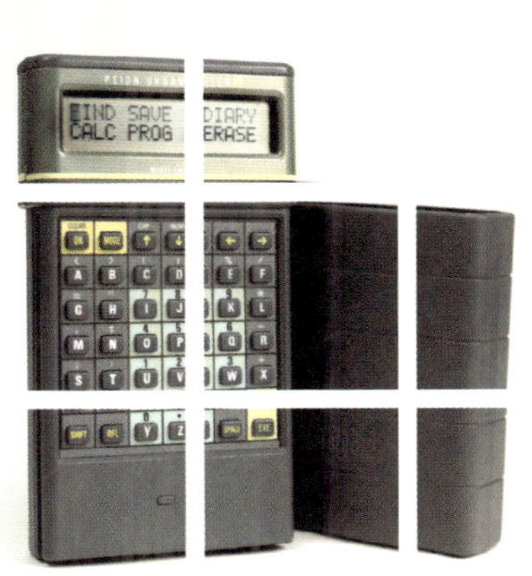

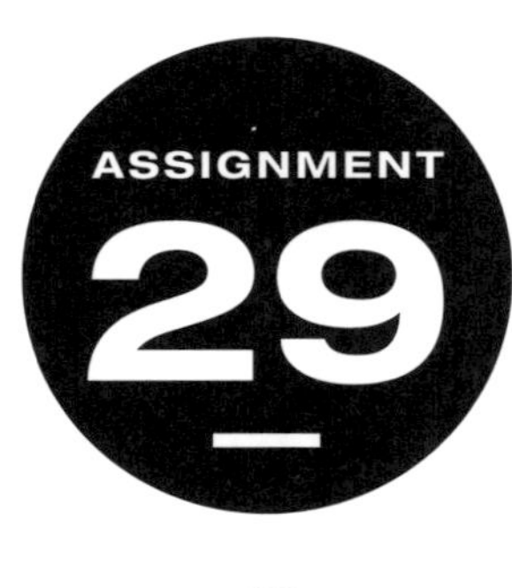

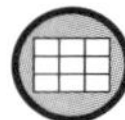

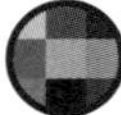

TECHNIQUE

When: Pick the light to reflect your story—natural daylight for hope, low light for a more gloomy mood.

Where: At home, in a place personal to you.

How: Look for mirrors or reflective surfaces such as glass windows, and capture a selfie or a part of your environment from an unusual angle. You can also try different types of mirror, such as those on vehicles.

Filters: Something a little dreamy, such as Amaro or Walden.

TAGS

#frame #mirror #photooftheday #feelings #life #quotes #portrait #selfie

MIRROR, MIRROR

Using a few simple props can transform your Instagram portraits and selfies, and one of the simplest and best is a mirror. You can use a mirror to create negative space in your picture, and to create optical illusions and multiple reflections, all of which will ask questions of the viewer and so keep their interest. The first part of your brief is simply to take a portrait or self-portrait, using a mirror to add intrigue. For a selfie, including your phone can be a clue to visitors that the caption is worth reading.

The joy of Instagram is that it allows you to instantly share what you see with a huge audience, and many people use their Feed to provide a window into their world. A mirror is a good way of signalling this. A clever combination of image and caption develops this relationship between viewer and photographer, and the second part of your assignment is to create an engaging caption for your best image. Try to write your image caption in the same way you would write a blog. Think about techniques that work well for bloggers, such as starting with a famous quote. Restrict yourself to one key point, give an example, and sum up with one sentence.

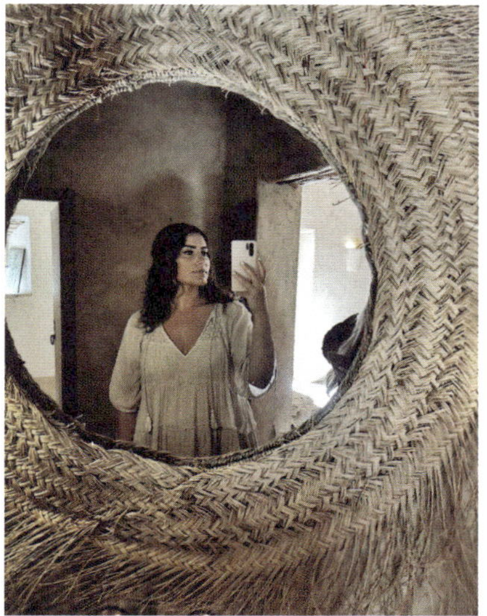

Nadia Meli
@nadiameli

<table><tr><td>

TIPS

You can also use a mirror to construct a humorous composition. It's worth leaving a mirror where your pet hangs out, and if it explores behind it you might be able to catch a two-headed (or headless) cat.

</td></tr></table>

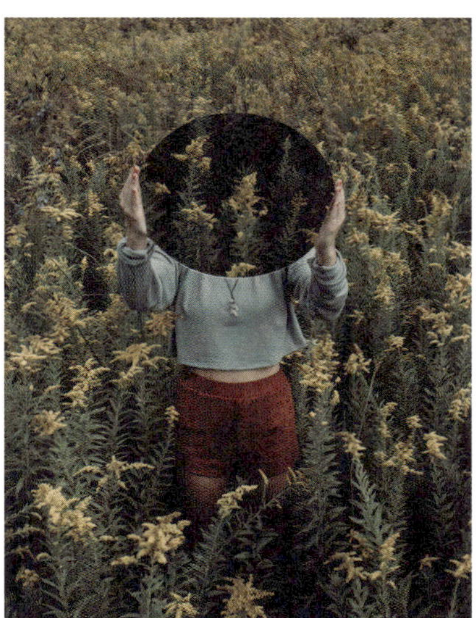

▲ You can use mirrors to create optical illusions that immediately have a sense of mystery and magic, and draw viewers into your photography.

Noah Buscher
@noahbuscher

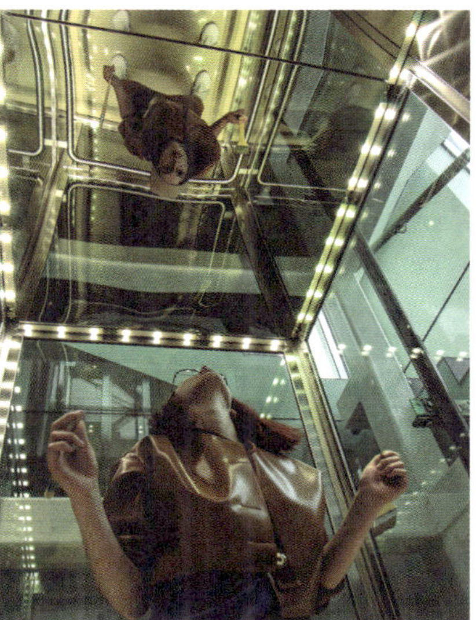

▲ Lights and mirrors can make for a fairground atmosphere, so keep an eye out for mirrors and polished glass that create multiple reflections.

Vale Zmeykov
@vale_zmeykov

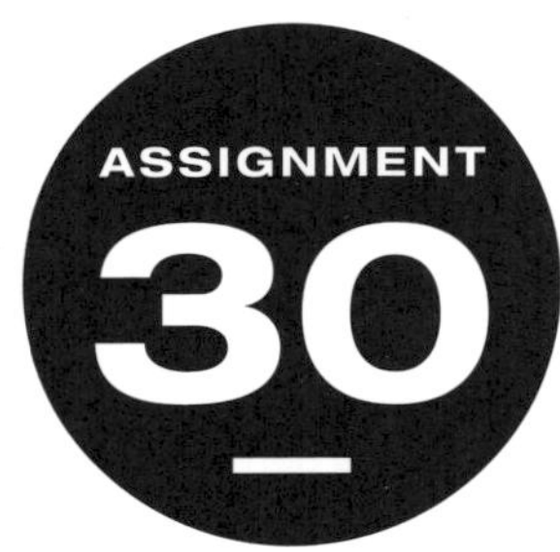

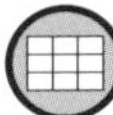

TECHNIQUE

When: Those fun and exciting moments in life.

Where: Anywhere you can find movement.

How: Use the Boomerang app to shoot and loop the action into a short, repeating movie.

Filter: Not really necessary.

TAGS

If you're not in Stories, add #boomerang into the mix (it has millions of followers).

BOOMERANG

Not all optical effects depend on your camera software. Some take advantage of the same principles as the smartphone long exposure (see Assignment 14) but can be achieved without leaving the Instagram world. The most well known is Boomerang, which shoots 10 images in quick succession and loops them back and forth, creating a fun animation that's a bit like a GIF.

If you don't already have the app, you can find the feature in the Stories section, although the dedicated app will create Boomerang loops for your Feed, too. These days, it's not something to go overboard with—when the feature arrived in 2015 people went mad and tended to overuse it—but just because it's had its 15 minutes of fame doesn't mean it's not still engaging.

Your assignment is to create a Boomerang. It's a great way to turn a momentary wonder into something that you and your Followers will want to linger on. You will need to find some movement that you can loop—examples that work well include fireworks, twirling dresses, jumping pets, and blowing kisses.

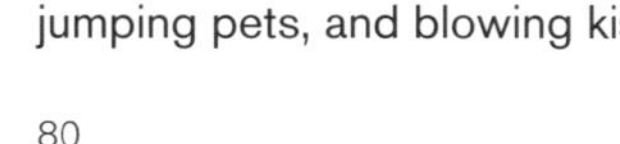

▼ *At a point of explosion in the stunning firework display held annually at #victoriapark in East London, Boomerang makes the rockets expand and contract endlessly in the sky—it's mesmerizing.*
Delightfully Peculiar
@delightfullypeculiar

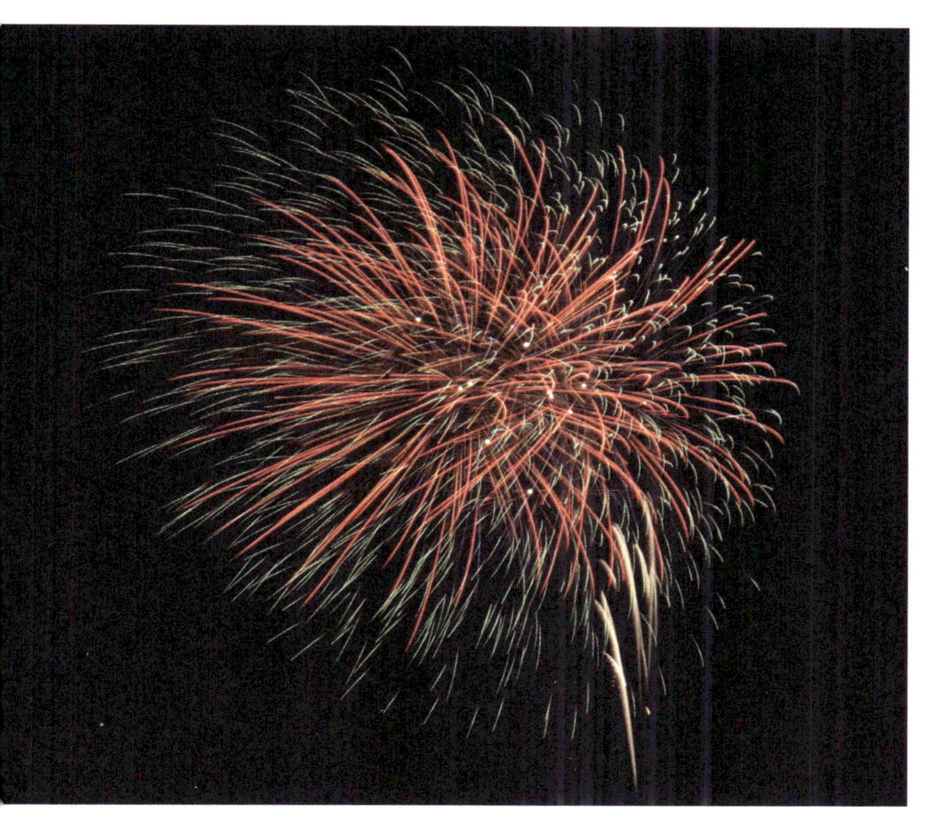

ASSIGNMENT 31

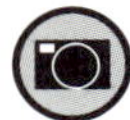

TECHNIQUE

When: On vacation, or when out and about.

Where: Anywhere you find action.

How: If you're editing for Stories, consider making each clip 15 seconds long and running several together.

Filters: Most video benefits from a bit of a contrast boost, so try Oslo or Tokyo.

TAGS

Don't forget to use Stickers to add a location and hashtags.

▼ *For this sequence, several minutes of video were cut down to just a few seconds using a video editing program, to show the most beautiful view and to zoom in and slow down at the moment of failure. Video doesn't zoom perfectly—you can see the grain—but it's only on screen momentarily.*

Adam Juniper
@juniperific

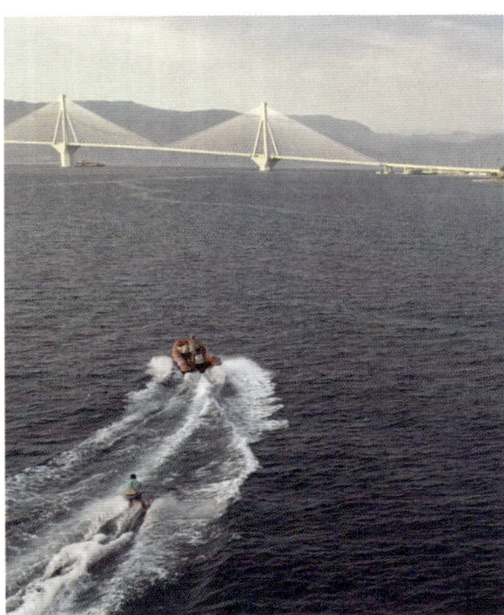

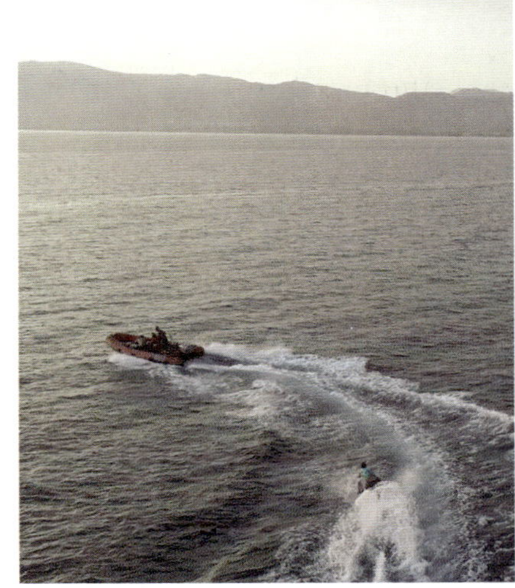

MINI MOVIEMAKER

IGTV is Instagram's answer to YouTube. It is a long-form video platform built into the app, which, like Stories, is built for vertical-format video. When you're creating a video for Instagram—either in Stories or IGTV—you might think that it's enough just to talk into the camera. However, for something that's going to stand the test of time, you're going to want to make your video slightly more special. Your brief for this assignment is not just to shoot, but also to edit, a video that does justice to your Feed.

Stories are limited to 15 seconds (although you can make more than one in sequence), but IGTV is not so restricted. Whichever you choose, set yourself the goal of creating something compelling using an editing program. This is probably best done on a computer, as phones have their limits and many phone editors lack lots of features. A desktop tool like iMovie will allow you to set the Aspect Ratio (the shape of the video) to the upright format favored by Stories and IGTV, which means you can crop and re-position any traditional landscape-format video for best effect.

You can extend this assignment into a video workshop by exploring how to create and edit an entire video in more detail in Assignment 50.

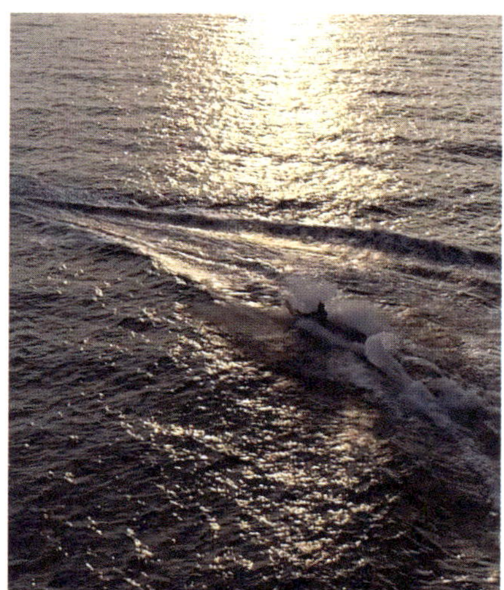

TIPS

- When you're shooting action video, capture at 60fps (frames per second) if possible, then you can slow it down to half-speed and it will still look smooth on screen.

- Patience is a virtue. After editing, the computer will process, or render, a single new video file. This takes time and is another reason a computer is better than a phone.

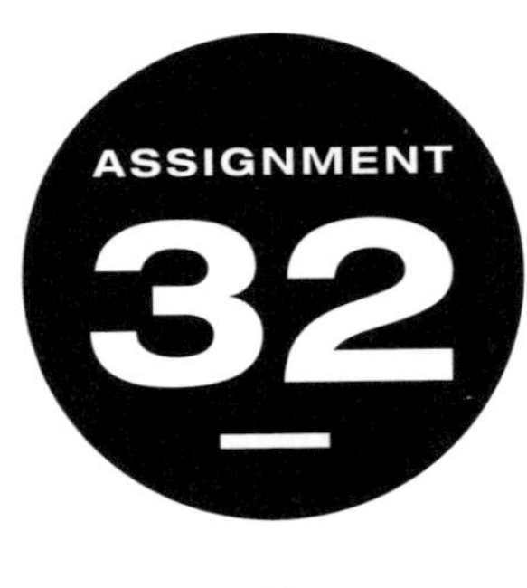

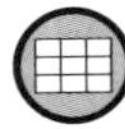

TECHNIQUE

When: Works well when background light is brighter than foreground light.

Where: Wherever you find yourself inside looking out.

Filters: In Edit, turn Saturation down and Contrast up.

TAGS

#window #pattern #abstract #light #blackandwhite #bnw #silhouette

▶ *A member of the Hikari Creative whose goal is to affirm the essential nature of art in our lives, Marina Sersale uses her smartphone to create artistic shots that are just as impressive as anything taken with a digital SLR. It proves that good technique and a creative eye are more important in photography than the equipment.*

Marina Sersale
@eauditalie

WINDOWS & FENCES

A great way to give a photograph texture and interest is to frame your subject through a window or barrier. For this assignment, keep an eye out for the perfect structure. The image by Marina Sersale shows exactly how to use this to create a great photograph. The window pattern and glass textures provide an intriguing foreground, through which you can just make out the two figures in conversation.

For the best effect, it really helps if your lens is flat-on to the window, but it's possible to fix any slight distortion with the Adjust option in Instagram's Edit menu. It's not obvious, but when you're in Adjust, a Crop button appears at the top right. Don't forget that moving forward and backward (and zooming in and out as necessary) will change the perspective, allowing you to reposition the distant subject in relation to the foreground.

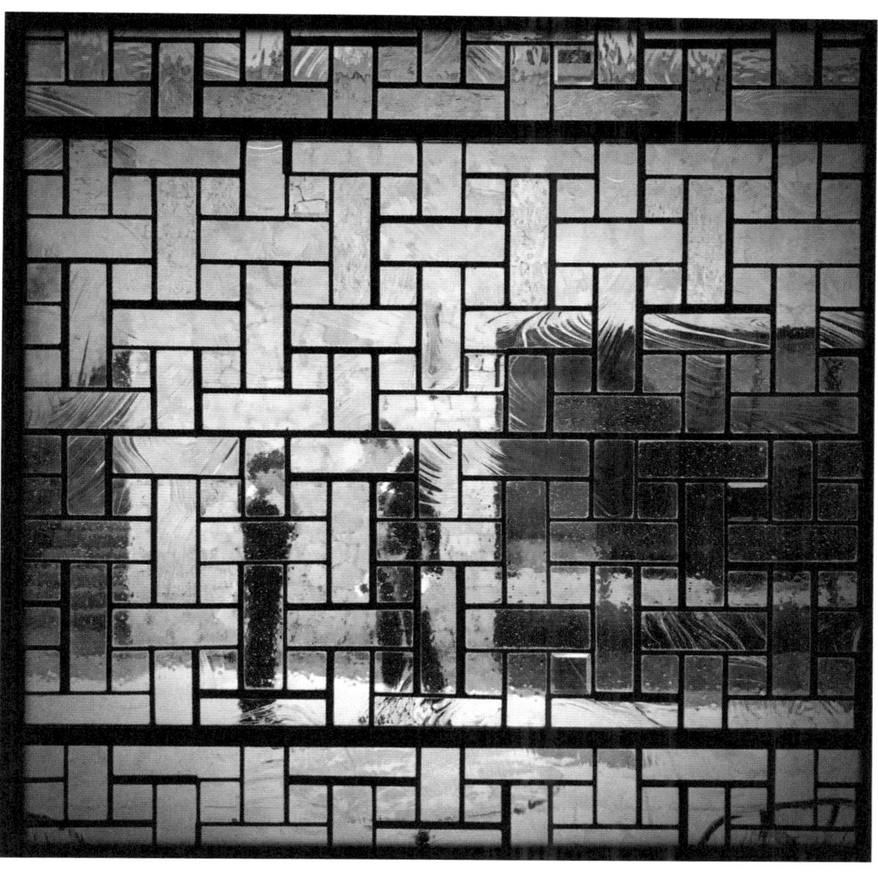

ASSIGNMENT JOURNAL

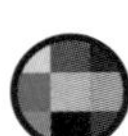

TECHNIQUE

When: Think in terms of multiple shots. Shoot at different times of day, as variations in lighting will add variety to your Feed.

Where: Wherever you travel—on vacation or on work trips!

How: Before you go, spend a bit of time exploring Google for possible essential shots, for example "Best Instagram Spots in [place name]." But don't let the results dictate all your images—look for different viewpoints as well.

Filter: Consider picking a consistent look for a trip—Aden is fun—but don't forget to use the Edit options as well.

TAGS

Make sure you include every location name you can think of, as well as the emoticons for the relevant flags.

#TRAVEL

It's not an exaggeration to describe Instagram as a highly competitive environment for travel photography. There are more than two billion photos a day being uploaded, and a significant proportion of those are travel-based. In the world of Instagram, there might be a good number more people viewing those images, so think of yourself a little like an advertiser—show viewers the world you're experiencing with panoramic photos and details of famous locations, and remember to use compositions that invite people into the scene. Showing a hand reaching backward is a slightly more original alternative to feet on a beach (or dangling off a cliff or building).

The next time you travel, your assignment brief is to capture your trip with the most bright, colorful, and intriguing shots you can achieve. Look for unusual angles of famous locations and, as well as posting as you go, consider using the "Combine your photos" option (selected via the uneven square-grid logo at the bottom of the photo upload screen) to create more elaborate layouts.

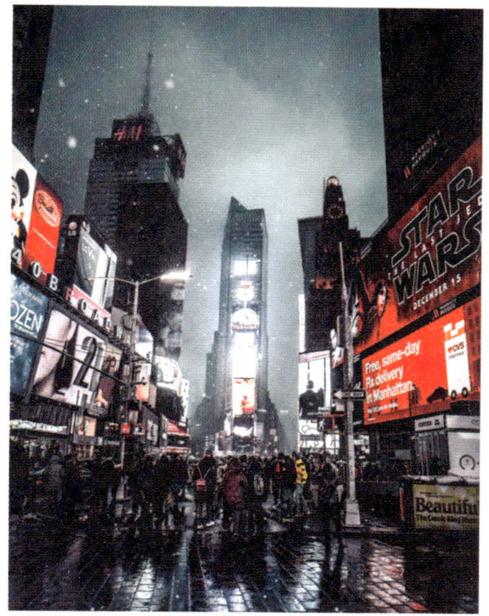

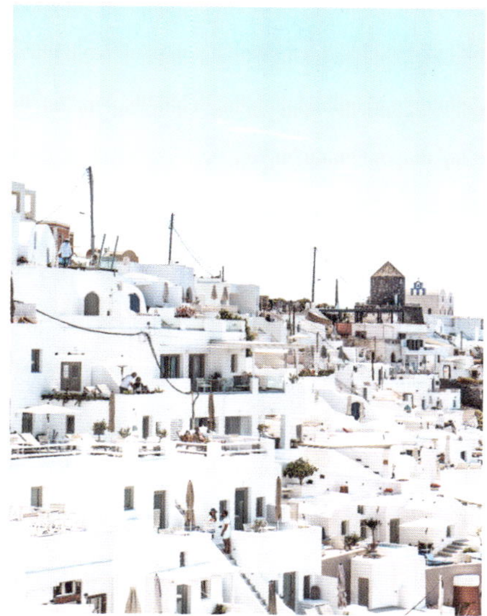

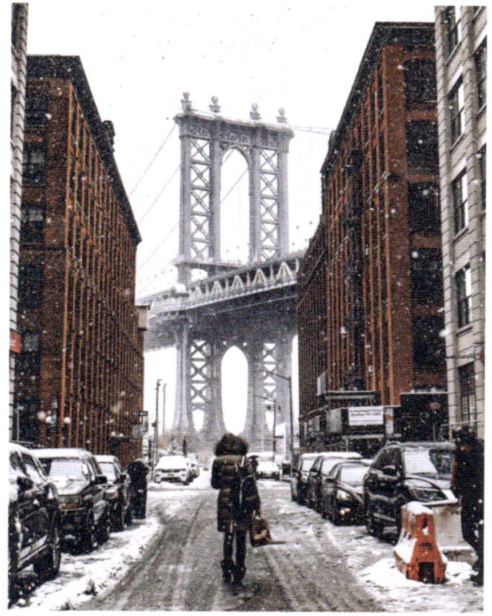

▲ *Photographer and record producer Andre Benz is not afraid to turn up the saturation and contrast, and has an eye for those classic (and enviable) scenes that might make great desktop backgrounds.*

Andre Benz
@benz

ASSIGNMENT JOURNAL

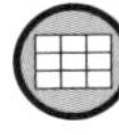

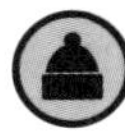

▶ Rock star, fashion photographer, author, and Nikon ambassador Dixie Dixon isn't just known for her camera skills. She is also something of a hat connoisseur, and you'll never find a selfie in her Feed that doesn't include one.

Dixie Dixon
@iamdixiedixon

TECHNIQUE

When: Ideally, whenever you're in shot.

Where: Hopefully your equivalent of Dixie's hat will be appropriate for all venues.

How: Show Followers what interests you.

Filter: You might choose to stick to a particular filter or style when you're in shot, too. For a commercial account, something as simple as editing all behind-the-scenes images in black and white can work.

TAGS

If you're sharing someone's products, tag their Feed using the Tag People function.

SHARE YOUR THING

It's not always easy to convey every aspect of your personality in a momentary image, but if there is something that matters to you, then make it matter to your Followers. For this assignment, set out to find something you're enthusiastic about and share it regularly on Instagram through your photography.

It could be your love of a color, flowers, cars, a musician, an artist—anything that tells people a little bit about yourself. The key here is to be consistent, which in turn means being genuine and sharing something that is true to you. This might involve a little bit of introspection, but consider that part of the brief. Then find a way to share that thing regularly in your images. You could even use it like an "Easter egg" in your pictures— by hiding a tiny toy in every shot. And if it's something you love, you can also write knowledgeably about your subject in captions again and again.

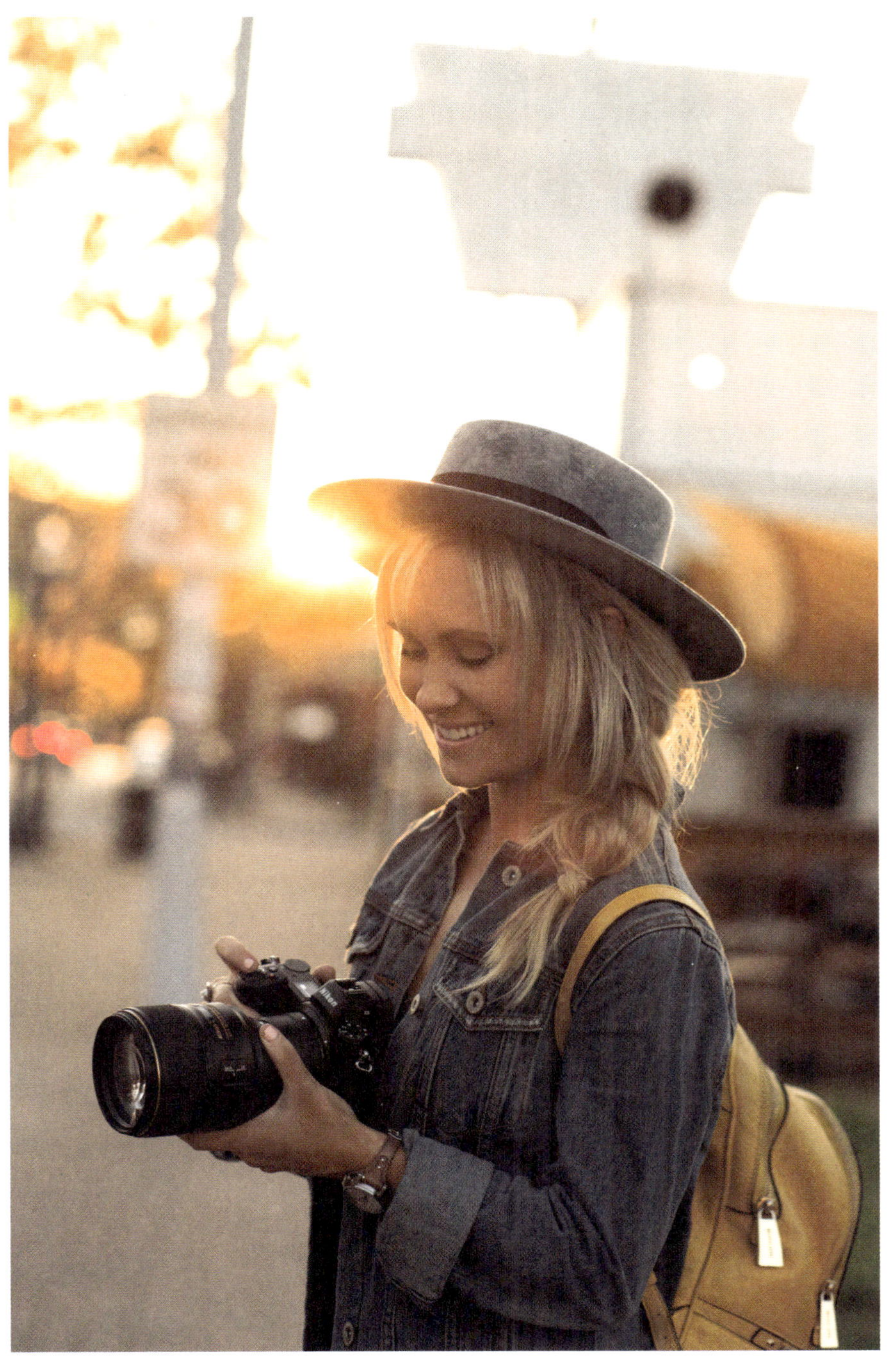

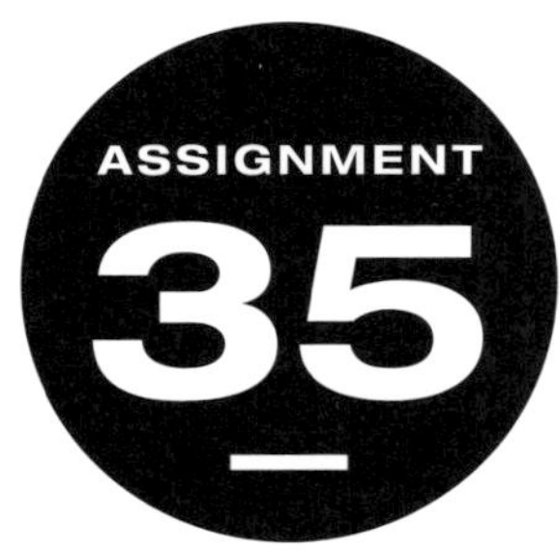

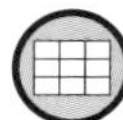

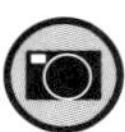

TECHNIQUE

When: In good light.

Where: Indoors, where you won't be disturbed.

How: Place your object against a plain backdrop and ensure it's well lit. Make sure you focus on the important part of the object, and experiment by shooting from different angles until you're happy with the image.

Filter: Juno and Ludwig will help lighten a white background out of existence.

TAGS

Once again, choose tags appropriate to your subject, but don't forget the context—if you're shooting earrings, for example, perhaps mention the kind of event they'd be worn to.

OBJECT LESSON

Photographing people is one thing—mostly, we instinctively know where to point the camera—but how can you consistently make objects look good? In this assignment, we're asking you to shoot an object attractively. It is well worth learning to do this effectively because one day you may want to sell what you're photographing; or because, at some point, you're going to want to show people something you're interacting with, and let your Followers into your world.

To take a picture of an object, decide what its focal point is, and make sure that the best available light is hitting it. Photographers use the term "hero shot" to describe the main image—they might need to capture images from every side of a product, but they'll also need to choose one creative angle as well.

To get a clean background, place a table next to a wall, then get a roll of white paper and tape it to the wall, allowing it to curve naturally onto the table. That way, there will be no sharp edge in your background. Don't forget to experiment with the Linear Tilt-Shift in Instagram's Edit page.

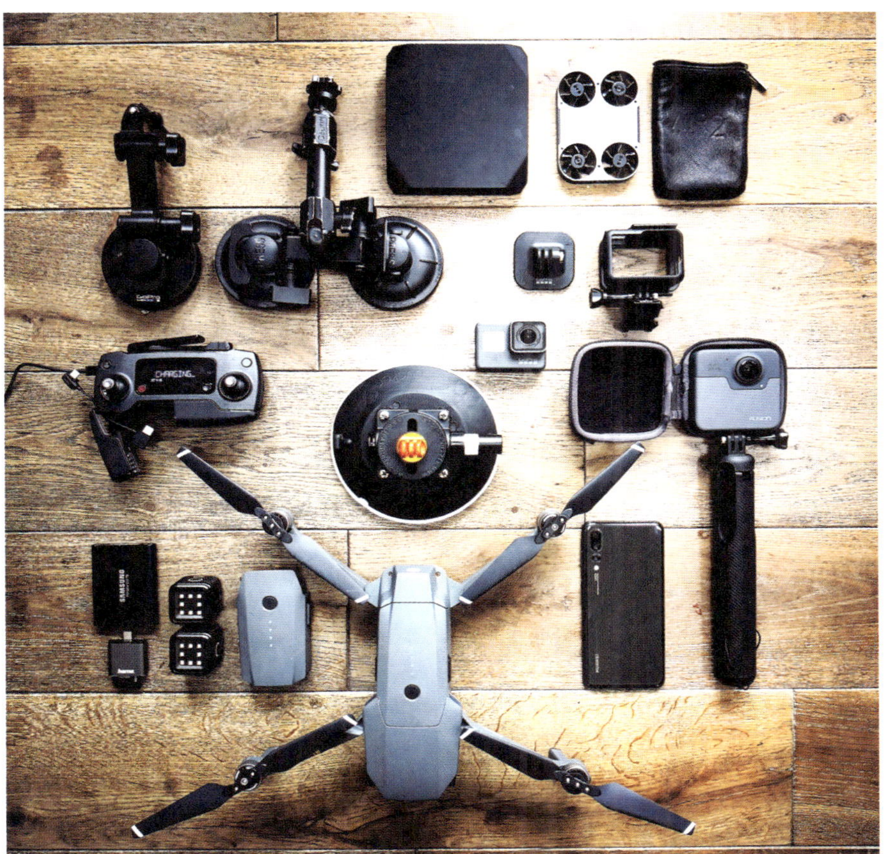

▲ *TV and social media content creator Jason Bradbury utilizes "flatlay" overhead photography to present a diagrammatic view of equipment such as this drone and camera gear required for a car shoot.*

Jason Bradbury
@jasonbradbury

ASSIGNMENT JOURNAL

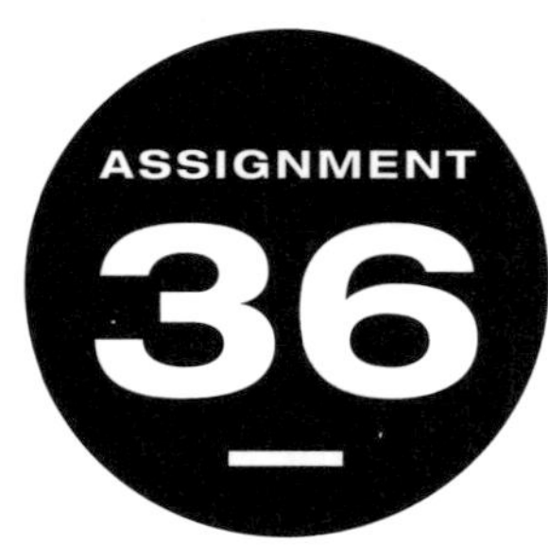

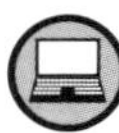
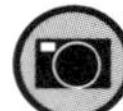
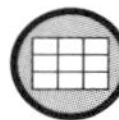

TECHNIQUE

When: Fast action benefits from good light.

Where: Somewhere awesome, obviously!

How: You can use a special camera or your smartphone to record the action, but remember to edit your video—or select the key stills—of your action sequence for posting as a Story.

Filter: Not necessary, but make sure the action is viewable, so tweak Brightness and Contrast if necessary.

TAGS

Remember to include names of participants, location, sport, and locations. And don't forget the brand of your action camera.

CAPTURE THE ACTION

The idea of immortalizing mad moments of glory (or carefully planned adventures) isn't new—the first GoPro came out in 2004—but action cameras now provide a firm alternative to risking your phone in wet or risky situations. Better still, the higher-end brands provide integration with your phone via Wi-Fi so you can plan a shot, activate the camera, and copy photos and video over without resorting to a computer.

To make the best of a moment of action, consider uploading a sequence—including an establishing shot that shows the whole scene and the moment of action itself. The leading brands provide attachments so you can put the action camera on top of your helmet, or even on your surfboard, to get the first-person view.

If you decide you're after a still photo (which might be even better quality), it's usually best to ensure you've got a generous amount of memory left on the camera's memory card, then use the timelapse mode to take a photo every second. For a jump from a waterfall, you should really use video—4K is still 8 megapixels. And don't forget that you can upload your edited video to Stories (see Assignment 22).

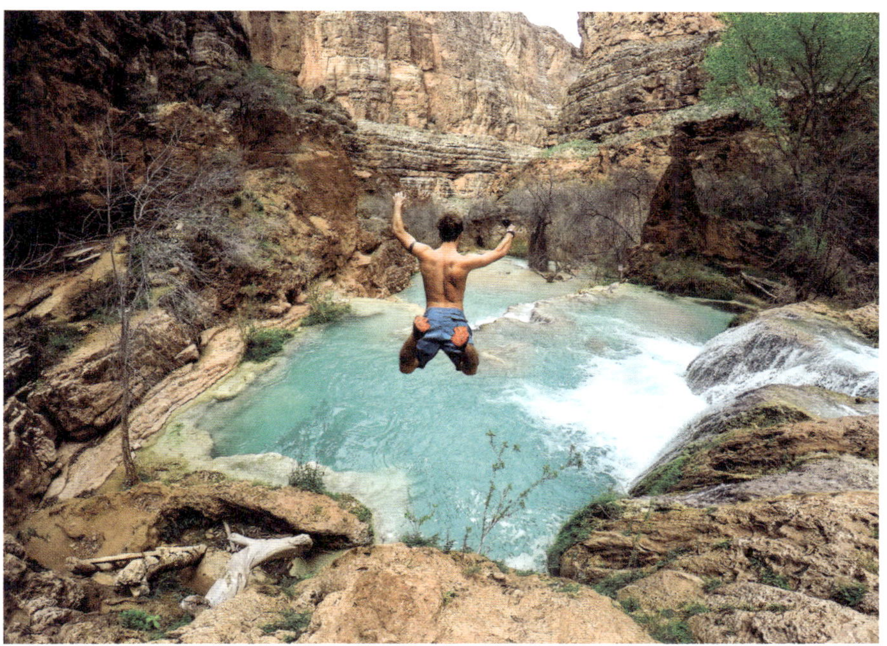

TIPS

- If you're going to be near water, make sure you keep your smartphone or camera dry using a specialist waterproof case!

- If you want to capture the action in slow-motion, you'll need to use a high frame rate. Normal digital video is shot at 30fps, but will look juddery when slowed down. Instead, shoot at 60fps and slow the sequence down to half the speed.

- Image quality can deteriorate because of the amount of information the processors in the camera can handle, so try to record at the highest bit rate you can—the higher the number in mega bits per second (mbps), the better.

▲ *Jeremy Bishop works as a commercial photographer who "seeks a blue state of mind." This shot shows a leap from height—a great wide view. The jumper has an action camera on a hand grip in his right hand.*

Jeremy Bishop
@bluumind

ASSIGNMENT JOURNAL

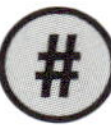

TECHNIQUE

When: Check your calendar and see what holidays are coming up.

Where: I prefer to do this where I have access to my photography archive.

How: Look for anniversaries and special dates in advance, and plan which of your images will best suit those days. Remember to post on the day using the day's hashtag.

Filter: Consider using an old image with a retro filter.

TAGS

Google "hashtag holidays" for an up-to-date calendar—new ones appear every year.

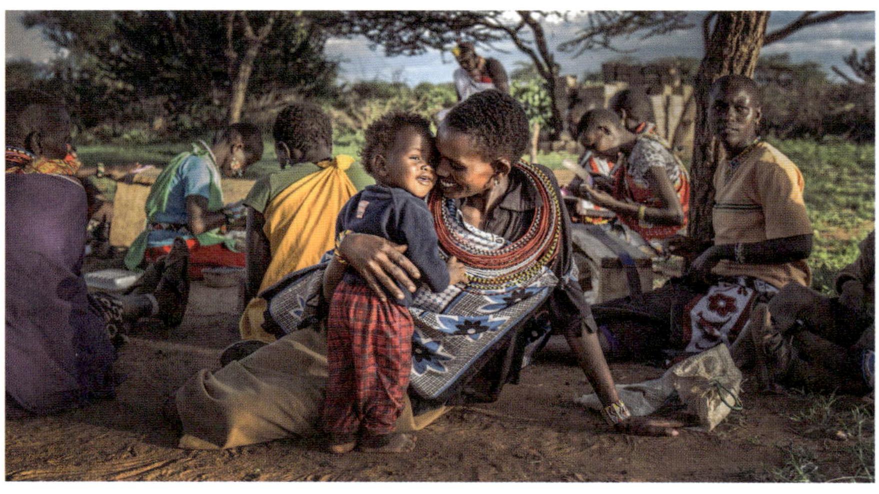

PERFECT TIMING

The time at which you post your photographs can have a huge effect on their impact, in terms of Likes and more nebulous factors. You can improve your Likes and Instagram algorithm score simply by posting at busy times of day, when more people are looking at Instagram, but you shouldn't forget to be seasonal, too.

This isn't just a cynical attempt to exploit the public mood, relentlessly pushed as it is by the commercial world—Christmas shopping, winter sales, Easter Shopping, Mother's Day, Father's Day, and so on. It's a really helpful way of concentrating your own mind—giving yourself a subject assignment to focus on, and a direction for your creativity. So, for this assignment, you should look up forthcoming special dates and post an appropriate image on each day—either new or from your archive—with the relevant hashtags, for as long as you can manage.

There are plenty of places to look for guidance, such as www.daysoftheyear.com, which keeps track of many special dates. There are often more than one per day as well—for example, 7 August is Lighthouse Day, Particularly Preposterous Packaging Day, and Aged Care Employee Day, among others. Whether these will strike the right chord is debatable, but there will be dates and events that prompt you to remember a particularly suitable image in your archive, or inspire you to capture an image to suit the occasion.

ASSIGNMENT JOURNAL

◀ *Posted on Mother's Day, this shot from Ami Vitale's assignment at the Loisaba Conservancy beautifully captures the mood of the day without shifting from her main work.*
Ami Vitale
@amivitale

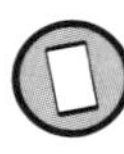

TECHNIQUE

When: Whenever you have some time to experiment with the look of your images.

Where: Where you have access to your camera archive.

How: Experiment with the suggested apps, and any others that you fancy. There is no substitute for spending a bit of time with each tool to get a feel for it.

TAGS

When you're editing images, don't forget to add the relevant tag for your app (for example, #photoshop) for a chance of being promoted by the app's developers.

FIND YOUR EDITOR

Finding your ideal image-editing app is a very significant assignment for any Instagrammer, as there will be times when you need more sophisticated software to edit your photos.

The first place to look is your smartphone's own software suite. Different manufacturers offer different solutions, but there are generally Edit options in your photo album. You can use these by taking a shot using your phone's camera app, editing it in the Library, then selecting the picture in Instagram—rather than shooting directly from Instagram.

Beyond that, there is a range of different apps that you can download—some free, some not—that will allow you to edit images in your catalog. These tools vary in sophistication, with plenty that will only handle a single task, such as adding a light-leak effect. To start with, experiment with the apps on the facing page.

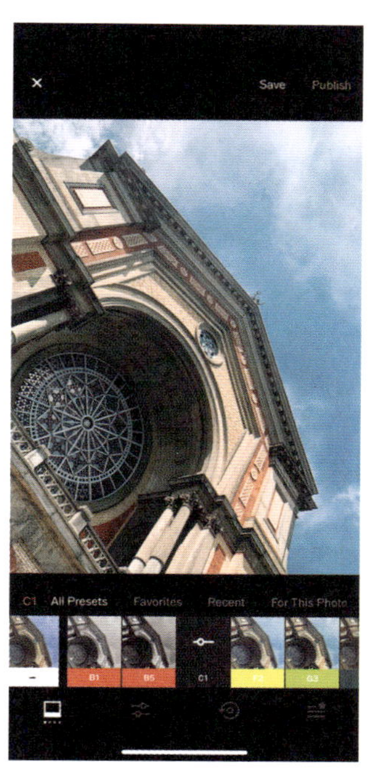

VSCO

◄ *Offers a good mix of presets and editing tools. It encourages you to join its own community, which is more like browsing an art gallery.*

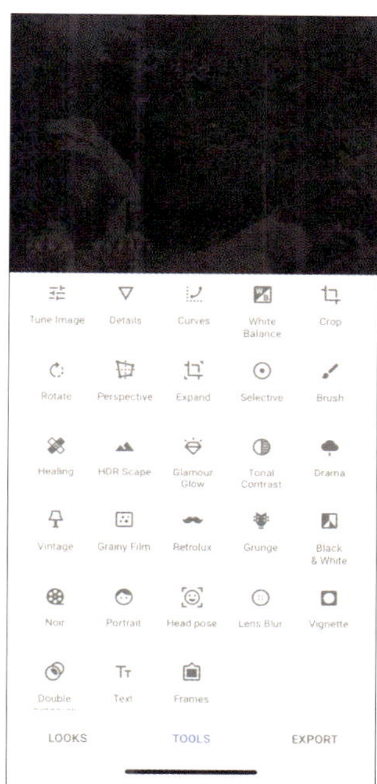

SNAPSEED

► *A Google app that includes a good selection of tools, such as Curves, which provides more control than Contrast.*

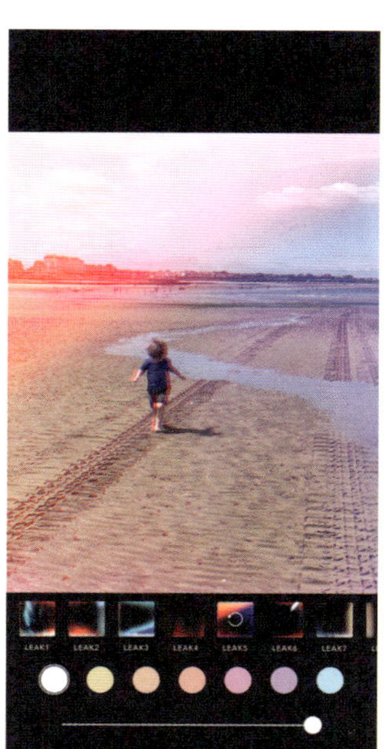

AFTERLIGHT

◄ *As well as a huge filter gallery, there's a complete array of pro tools, including Curves, double exposures, plus color-shift and light-leak effects.*

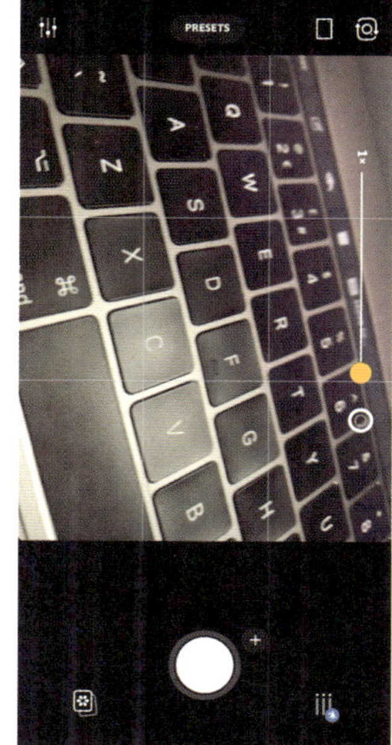

CAMERA+ 2

► *A popular app because it can handle Raw images and works seamlessly between Apple's iPhone and iPad devices.*

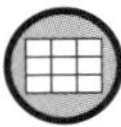

TECHNIQUE

When: Morning rush hour gives you lots of chances for interactions, and morning light is good for photographing people.

Where: Head for city streets, stations, shopping malls, and tourist attractions to maximize your chances.

How: Keep looking and waiting, and be ready with your camera set to Burst (or Live Photo) mode.

TAGS

#streetphotography #decisivemoment

CAPTURE THE MOMENT

The famous street photographer Henri Cartier-Bresson spoke of capturing the "decisive moment." Anticipating how people are going to behave, and being ready to photograph them, may seem difficult at first, but it is a skill that can become instinctive with practice, and it can produce pictures that attract a lot of Likes.

The key to capturing the decisive moment, among friends or strangers, is to be always on the lookout. You don't ever quite know what, when, or who will provide this moment until you see it. Try to put yourself at the heart of events where there will be opportunities—celebrations, festivals, or protests, for example—and keep watch. Monitor situations as they develop, such as a street artist or performer presenting their act, or someone giving a speech, and look for people's reactions. The best photograph is not always found center stage. Your brief is to capture a decisive moment of emotion or humor that will attract comments to your Feed. Post your "decisive" single image from a particular event, and take note of the response.

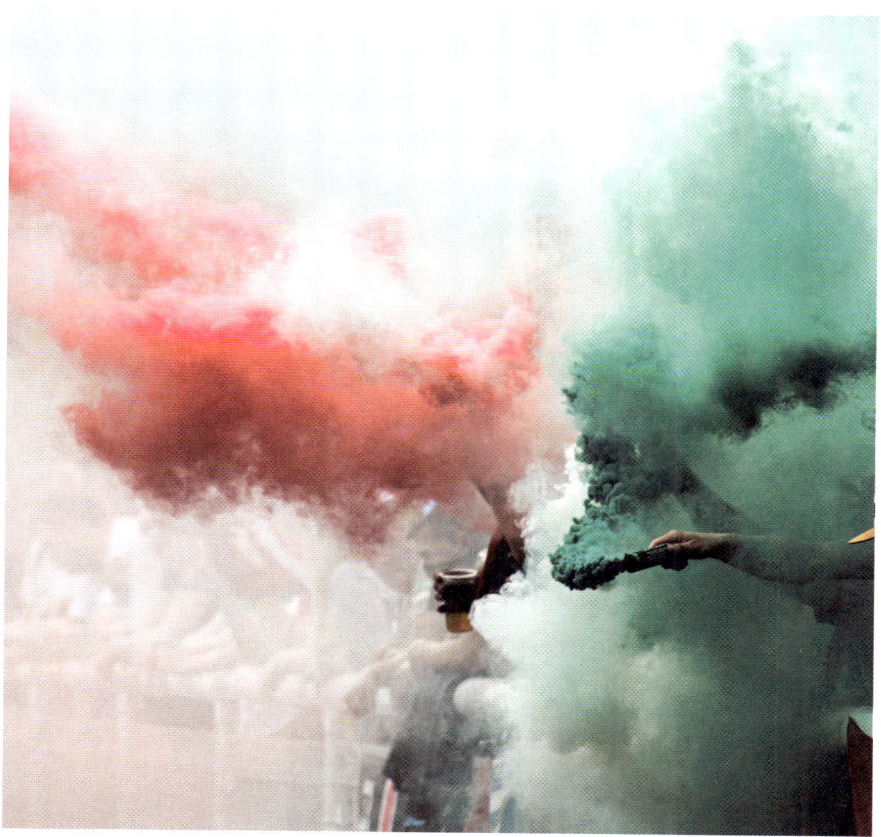

TIPS

- An increasing number of professional street photographers are using smartphones, as they're small and discreet, and enable you to photograph people without being noticed.

- This is another assignment that cries out for enabling the Burst mode (or Apple's Live Photo) on your smartphone, so the camera fires multiple shots. You can select the one that captures the "decisive moment" later.

▲ *Seamus Travers is a street photographer with an eye for unusual situations. Here, he was shooting at the CONIFA World Cup (a soccer tournament for countries that aren't recognized by FIFA), and his eye was naturally drawn to the drama and color of the smoke grenades.*
Seamus Travers
@treamo

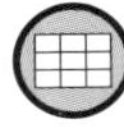

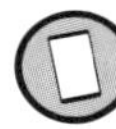

TECHNIQUE

When: Daytime with thin cloud—for diffuse lighting—helps you to capture reflections without bright spots that obscure the image.

Where: Anywhere you find water—puddles, ponds, or lakes—or glass.

How: Look for reflected images in glass windows or doors, or in a still lake or a puddle on the sidewalk with flat, reflective water.

Filter: You'll need to shoot outside Instagram and flip the image in a specialist image editor app (such as Snapspeed or Quickflip), after which you can add it to Instagram and post.

TAGS

#flip #reflection #reflect #water

REFLECT & FLIP

In the never-ending quest to make viewers give our Feed the second glance that might lead to a Like, we've seen the power of a carefully composed reflection (see Assignment 29). However, if you add a very basic piece of image manipulation to your image you will have a whole new trick up your Instagram sleeve.

Strangely, at the time of writing there is no option to flip a photo in Instagram. You can crop and rotate, and even adjust the perspective, but being able to flip an image like a mirror (which is a less computationally complex process) is not an option. That's no problem, though, as you can easily get another app to do it.

To complete your assignment, compose a photograph so that the reflection is the main subject, then flip it. Shoot a variety of reflections and experiment with flipping them round in this way, then post the best for your viewers to reflect upon.

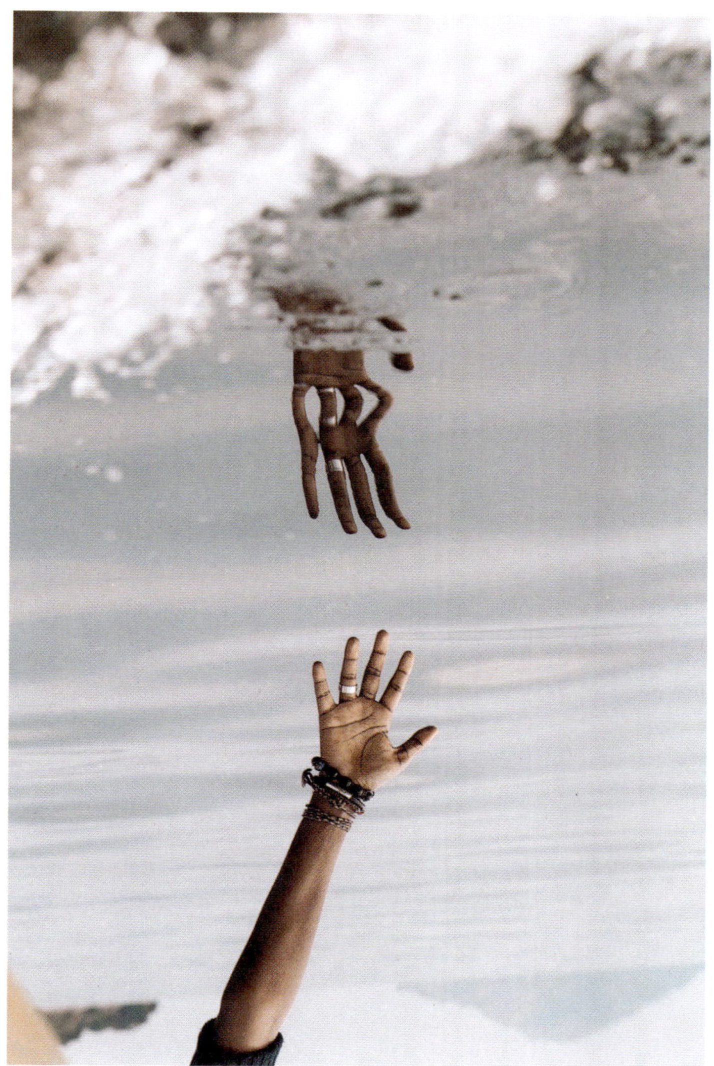

▲ *This surreal image by Serrah Galos of a hand and its distorted reflection in water has been made all the more intriguing by flipping it through 180 degrees.*

Serrah Galos
@rwanda_nziza

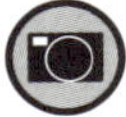

TECHNIQUE

When: Anytime you feel you need inspiration.

Where: Out of your comfort zone.

How: Forget about Likes and Followers, and experiment with your photography.

Filters: Try lots of new ones, and make changes to your images that you've never made before.

TAGS

#creativephotography #experimentalphotography #abstractphoto #contemporaryphotography

▼ ▶ *These shots by Swedish photographer Jens Johnsson show contrasting views of the world.*

Jens Johnsson
@jens_johnsson

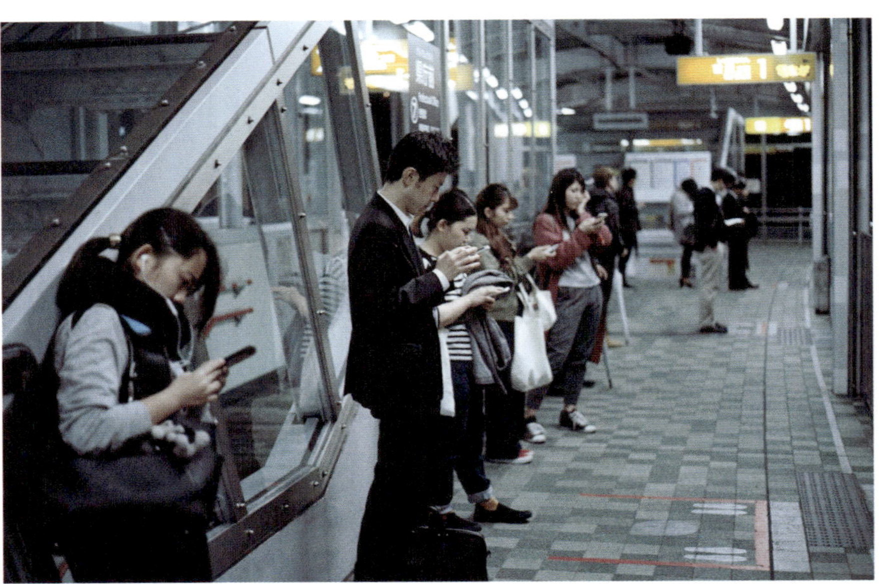

FIND YOUR MOJO

Even those of us who are passionate about the value of Instagram accept that it's very easy to get addicted to the thrill of accumulating Followers and Likes. Sometimes, it's a good idea to take a step back and remember the thrill of joining Instagram in the first place. After all, the chances are that you—like me—were drawn to it because of its focus on photography, and because you love creating and being inspired by great images. For this assignment your brief is to forget about hashtags and rediscover your own creativity. Put down your smartphone, pick up a camera, and try one or more of the following to find your mojo:

- Discover a new environment. It doesn't have to be far away, but if you're used to photographing landscapes, for instance, immerse yourself in a city instead.
- Take a crash course in a form of photography you've not tried before, such as macro, sports, or documentary. Take as many images as you can in a single weekend.
- Spend some time using just one lens on your camera.
- Shoot only in black and white, or in a square or panoramic format, or on film.
- Experiment with long exposures (see Assignment 14).

Transfer the results to your smartphone, and use Instagram filters that you haven't used before to edit your images. You might discover a whole new photographic style that reignites your passion for Instagram.

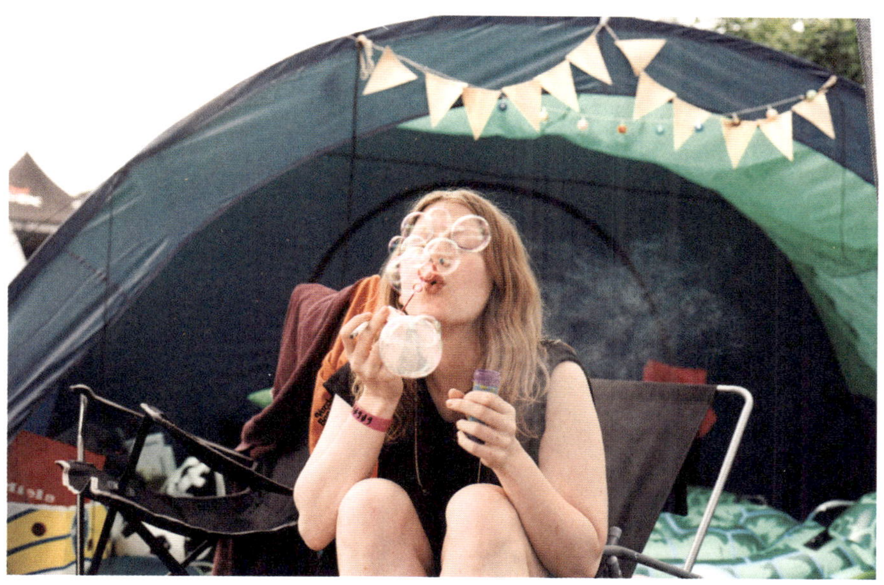

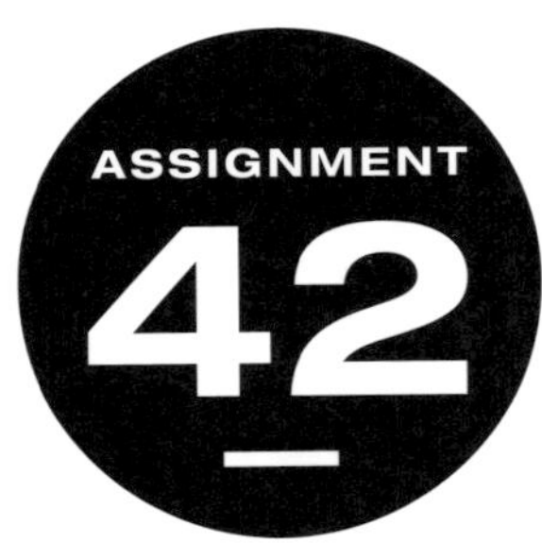

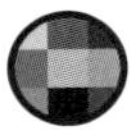

TECHNIQUE

When: In the evening or at night.

Where: This works well indoors with reflections from different lights.

How: You'll need friends with smartphones. Turn the flashlight mode on (on an iPhone this can be done from the unlock screen). Direct your friends to aim their smartphones so you get the look you want.

Filters: Smartphone LEDs aren't very bright, so try using an app with a Curves tool to adjust the brightness levels of your shot.

TAGS

#lighting #mood #pocketstudio

POCKET LIGHTING

Carefully altering the light from different sources around the subject is an important technique in portraiture, and many studio photographers use an expensive array of equipment. But you can actually achieve impressive lighting effects with quite simple set-ups. For this assignment you will create a flash portrait with nothing more than a little help from your friends—and the lights on their smartphones.

Flash photography using cameras with built-in flashes is never ideal, as the subject closest to the camera will be bathed in flat light that "falls off" very quickly, while the background disappears into darkness. In a studio, photographers avoid this by lighting the subject slightly from the side, which reveals the shape of the face. They might also light from the other side at a different brightness so that there is still detail in the darker areas. The color of the lights can be manipulated by covering them with colored "gels."

To create your pocket-lit portrait, position some friends with their phones in flashlight mode around your subject. Have one of them come in close to get as much light as you can on one side of the face, while the other holds their light about twice the distance away on the opposite side. With a little experimentation, you should be able to turn the darkest setting into a makeshift portrait studio. Post your best shots.

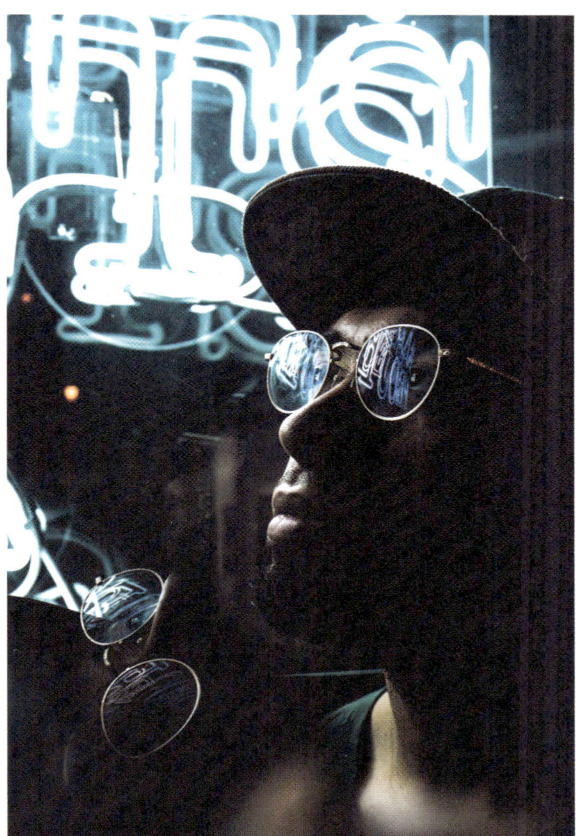

Drew Graham
@dizzyshotit

> ## TIP
>
> Whatever light source you use, it's always useful to be able to supplement it with a reflector—a white or pale surface that reflects light back onto the subject. You can buy cheap, foldable ones, or even use a white sheet, board, or piece of foam.

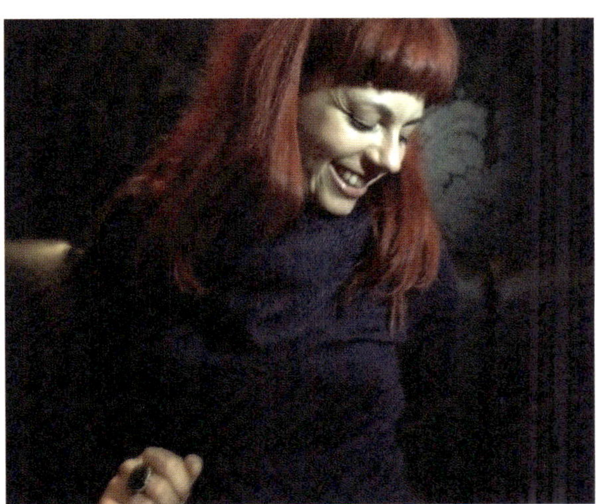

Adam Juniper
@juniperific

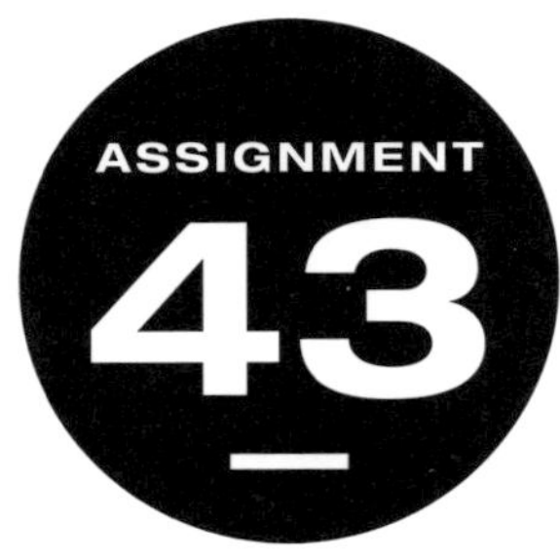

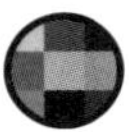
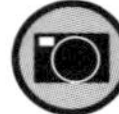

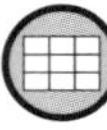

TECHNIQUE

When: In good light, using daylight through a window for some directional light.

Where: Somewhere your pet is relaxed.

How: Make sure your pet is engaged, with plenty to do, then turn on Burst mode (Live Photo on Apple's iPhone) to help you capture the right moment. Remember to look for the catchlight in the eyes!

Filter: Clarendon or anything that increases contrast, saturation, and sharpness.

TAGS

#pet #love #intheeyes

▶ *Alice van Kempen, who explores urban ruins with her bull terrier Claire, uses natural light (and Claire's uncanny ability to sit very still) to create fine art images reminiscent of Old Masters.*

Alice van Kempen
@alicevankempen

#PET 1: LIGHTING

Never work with animals, they say, but for the next two assignments that's exactly what you're going to do—by shooting a pet portrait. Obviously, even the most cooperative pet is not always going to follow your directions, but you can work to create the optimum conditions and then take multiple shots to ensure you capture the best moment. Of course, that's the magic of digital cameras and Instagram—you have the option of only posting the one that comes out right.

The first key to success is lighting. One very simple rule is to work with plenty of daylight. As long as there isn't direct sun, this should give you a soft and pleasing light. Also aim to capture a "catchlight" in the animal's eyes, which will add character (without catchlights, eyes can appear glassy and lifeless). Ensure backgrounds complement the subject, or alternatively crop out or blur distracting elements. You can add studio lighting, but that is one more element that might go wrong!

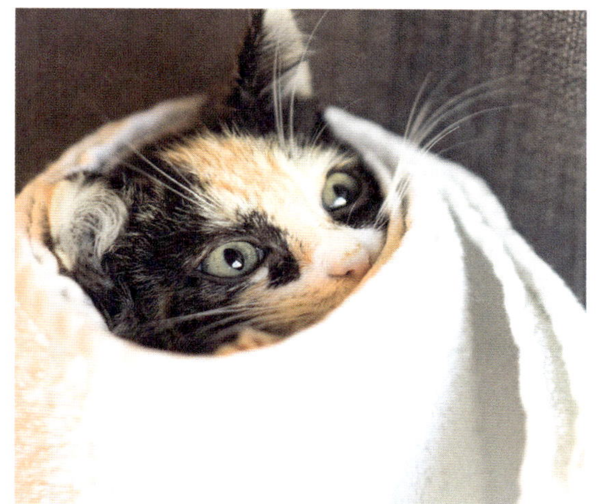

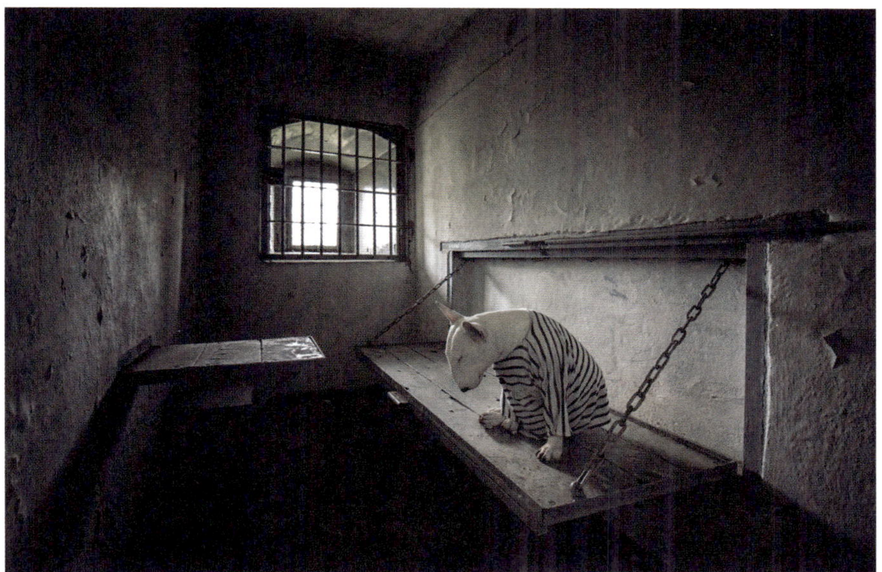

TIP

Some smartphones give you the option of selecting the exact moment from a series of photos they shoot in Burst mode—this is called Live Photo on iPhones. Look for it in your phone's instructions and, if it's available, make use of it. The software is often smart enough to capture the best smile and open eyes with humans, but it might struggle with animals, so there's a better chance you'll find the best shot if you check manually yourself.

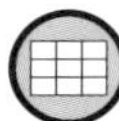

TECHNIQUE

When: When your pet is happy and relaxed; good light is important again.

Where: At home or in familiar surroundings, such as the local park.

How: Be on the look out for special moments, and keep Burst mode set. Or make your own moments with props, toys, and treats!

Filter: Whether you use no filter or something dramatic, use it consistently to reflect the tone you want your images to convey.

TAGS

Mention the specific (#puppy, #dog) and the general (#petsofinstagram #instadog #cute).

#PET 2: COMPOSITION

It's always raining cats and dogs on Instagram, but learning to shoot a well-lit pet portrait is only the first step toward standing out from the pack. Creating strong compositions with a distinctive personality (and going beyond simply the personality of your pet) is the second key to attracting a devoted following.

Your assignment brief is to compose images with a "pet personality." Humor is always a popular option, and this might begin with the appearance or behavior of your subject. You can enhance this by using a particular prop, photographic style (such as black and white) or compositional approach (such as extreme close-ups). Backgrounds are another important tool, and creating your own illustrated backdrops is a fun way to go. Whatever approach you take, compose a series of pet portraits with a consistent theme or tone, and add one daily to your Feed. Posting regularly (throwing your audience a bone) is vital to your success.

TIP

Watch for animals' expressions and poses that look or can be interpreted as "human"–like crossed legs, a paw over the face, a smile, surprise–and match your hashtag to the pose when you post it.

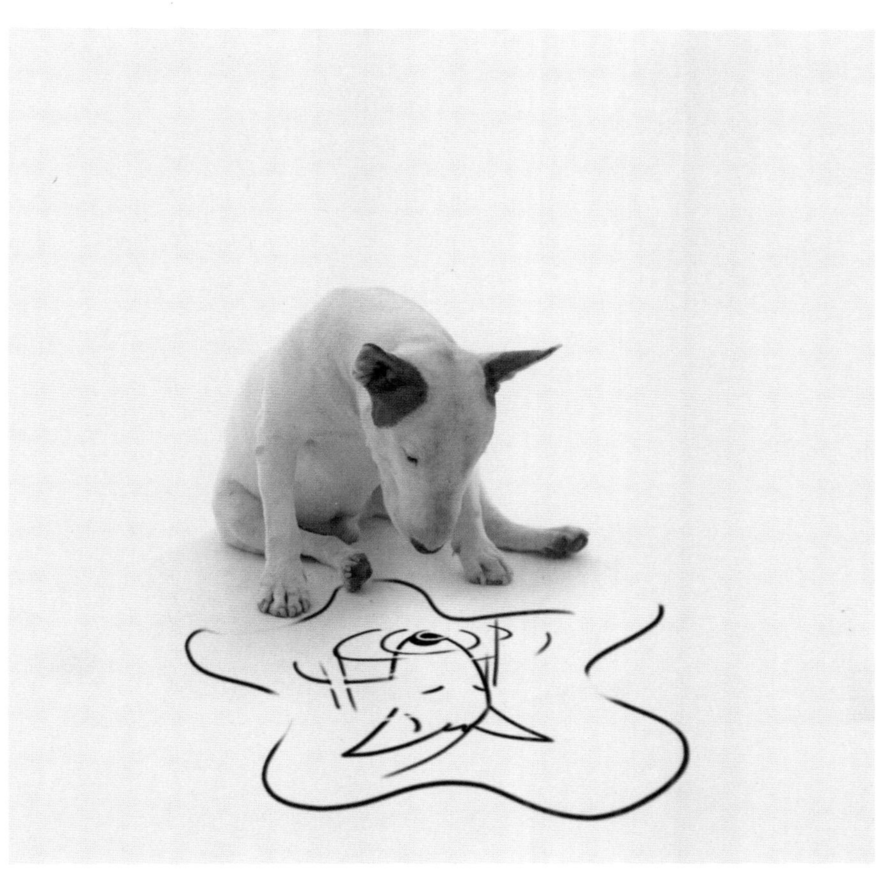

ASSIGNMENT JOURNAL

▲ *With his inspired idea to use a marker pen to draw an imaginary world around his bull terrier, Jimmy Choo, Rafael Mantesso created a Feed that became both a social media sensation and the bestselling book,* A Dog Named Jimmy.

Rafael Mantesso
@rafaelmantesso

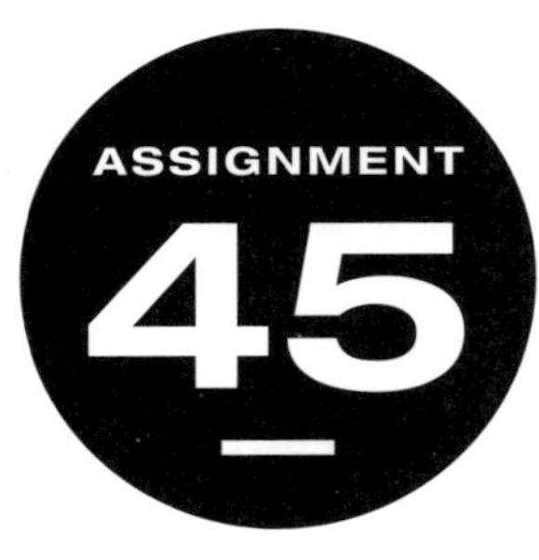

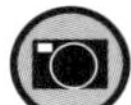

TECHNIQUE

When: Any time you're dealing with strong lighting from one source, for instance on sunny, cloudless days or when indoors.

Where: The less "normal" your composition, the less your smartphone app's artificial intelligence will be able to help.

How: On your smartphone, place the focus point manually to select the important area in the composition to ensure it's not too light or dark. On a camera, use your exposure metering to precisely control the area you're exposing for.

TAGS

Tags depend on the subject (#specialmoment, #halo), but if you're taking control of the exposure, you can also use photographers' terms (#backlit, #exposure, #manual).

TAKE CONTROL

It's easy to forget in these days of super-smart smartphones that a camera has its limits, and when it reaches them you need to take control and offer some help. Smartphone software looks for faces and attempts to adjust exposure accordingly. It also measures the bright and dark areas, and averages them out. This can mean that when you're getting good detail in the darker areas, the brightest areas become "blown" or overexposed.

Sometimes, you can make better choices than your camera. With most smartphones, this is very easy. Simply tap on your subject on the screen. This is often enough to assert yourself over the software's artificial intelligence (AI), informing it what to prioritize and how to expose the shot. If that doesn't do the trick, you can either adjust the on-screen brightness if your phone gives you the option, or adjust the Exposure in the camera's Expert mode.

For this assignment, set out to push your smartphone's AI to its limits—by shooting into the light, for instance—and experiment with controlling the exposure. If you are using a digital SLR, take control by switching from Auto to Manual mode.

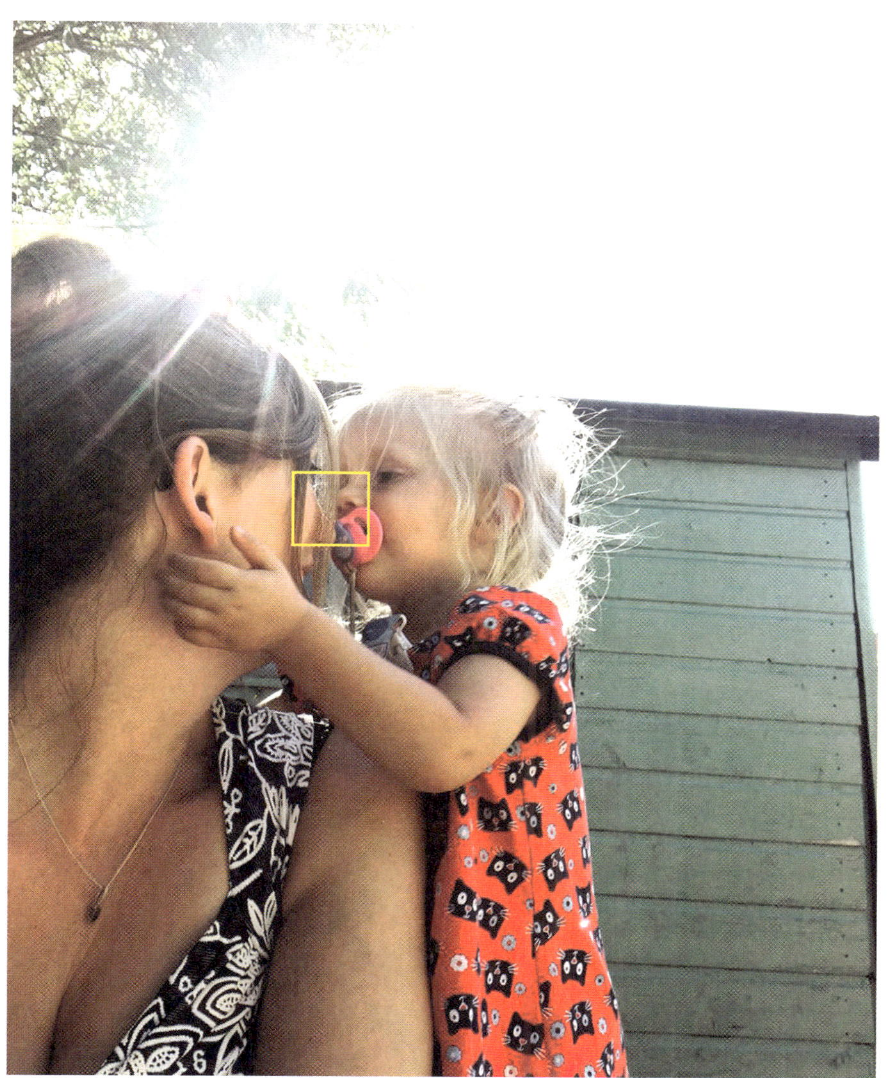

▲ Since mother and daughter are looking at each other, the camera's AI doesn't "see" their faces. Without help from the photographer, the image would have shown detail in the sky, but dark subjects. Instead, focus and correct exposure were achieved by placing the focus point (the square on the picture) on the faces. Placing the sun behind the tree would have helped to control the glare more, but the back-light on the subjects' hair enhances the image.

Amy Pepper
@prettywigspattikin

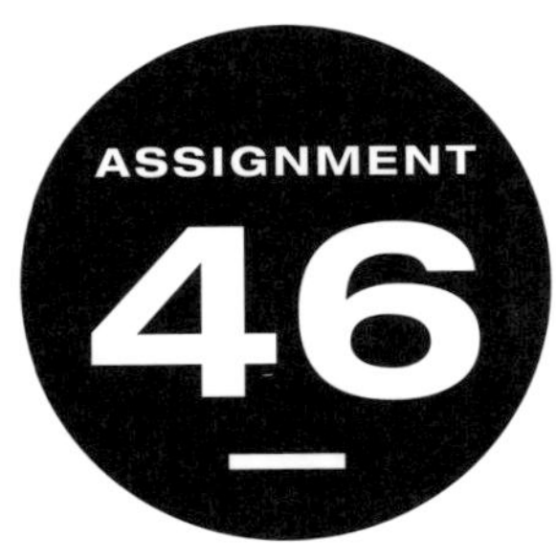

TECHNIQUE

When: At regular intervals.

Where: Wherever you can set up a shot with your storyboard or device.

How: Pick a relevant device and stick with it. Set a reminder on your phone to make sure you take photos at exact intervals, and post them as soon as you can.

TAGS

#baby #(number)months #(number)monthsold #growing

SIGNPOSTS

While many people love new storytelling features such as Stories, the standard Feed remains popular. It is still possible to use it for regular posts that keep your Followers informed, particularly if you use a method of sharing progress that is easily repeatable. That is what this assignment is all about. Although you can now add text to an image separately in Instagram, you can be a little more creative by adding text within the photograph itself. Storyboards or chalkboards, which are easily found in gift stores, offer a fun way to insert text into your image. Remember to ensure that the key information you write on the board is sufficiently large to be visible even when viewed at thumbnail size on your Feed.

Arrange your storyboard, or whichever device you decide to use to communicate your message each time, and capture a photograph of your main subject to post on your Feed at suitable intervals. If you're following the growth of your baby, for instance, once a month seems ideal. When your Followers scroll back through your Feed, the simple images will provide a consistent style and clear signposts that give an impression of time passing.

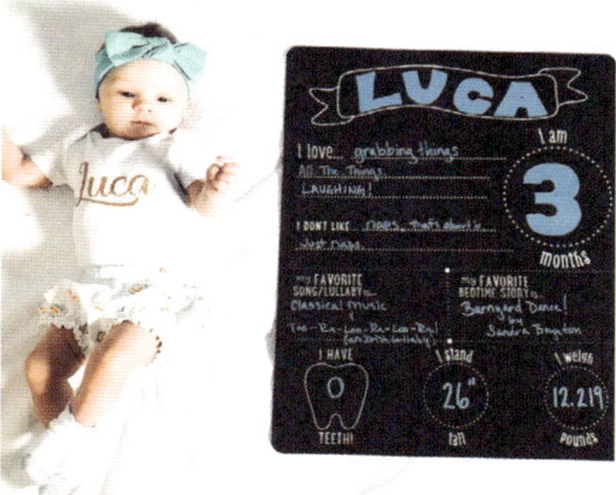
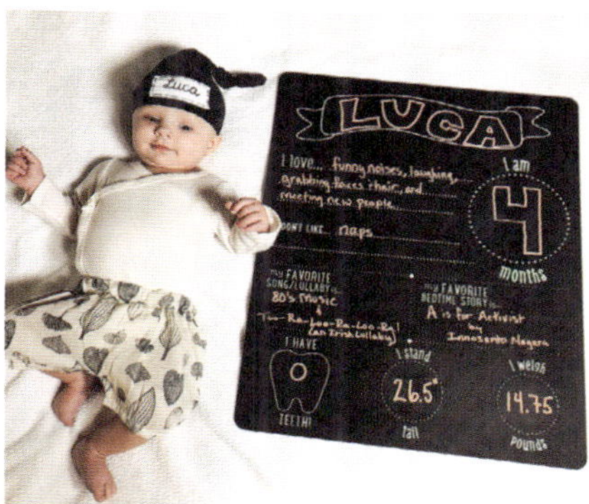
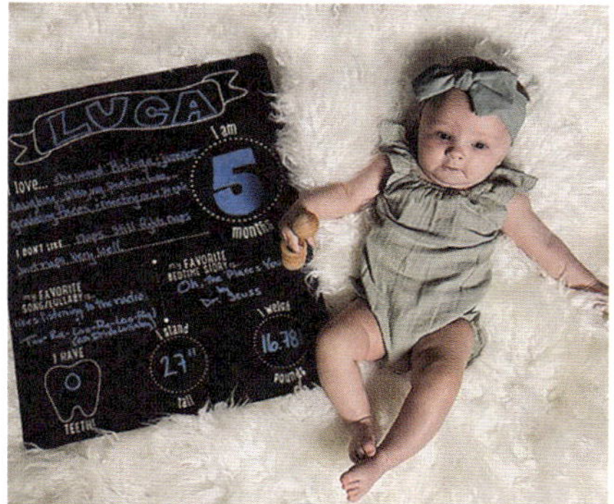
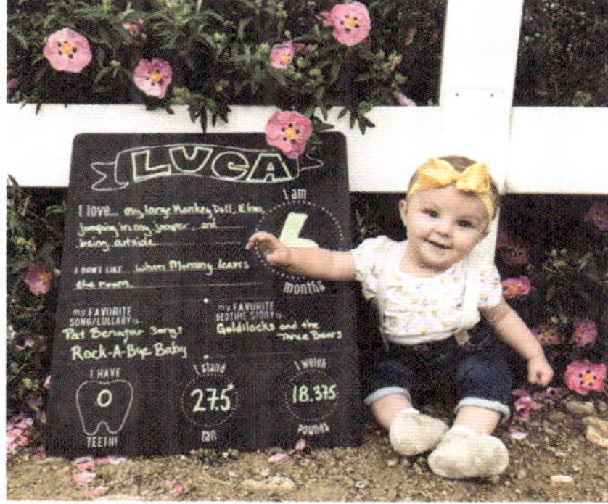
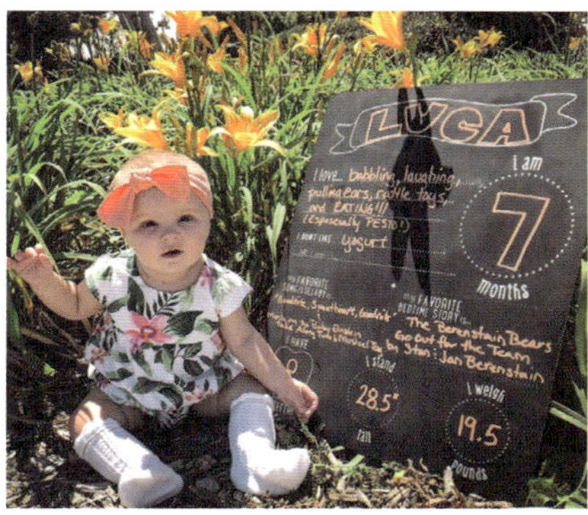
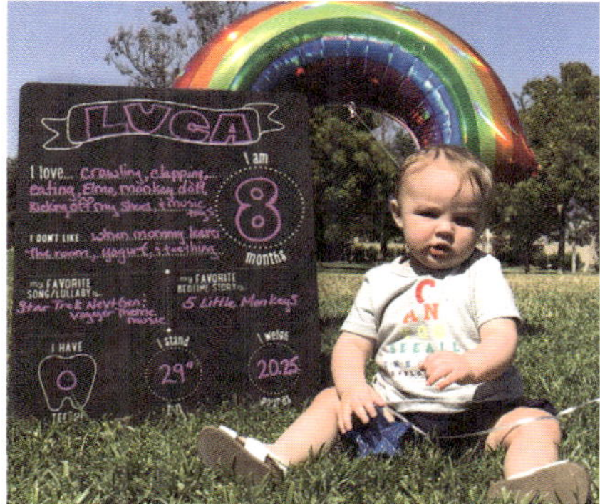

▲ *A filmmaker who shares her time between Los Angeles and London, Chris Sherwood has been documenting the progress of her daughter @Luca_sherwood using a storyboard device.*

Chris Sherwood
@csherwoodfilm

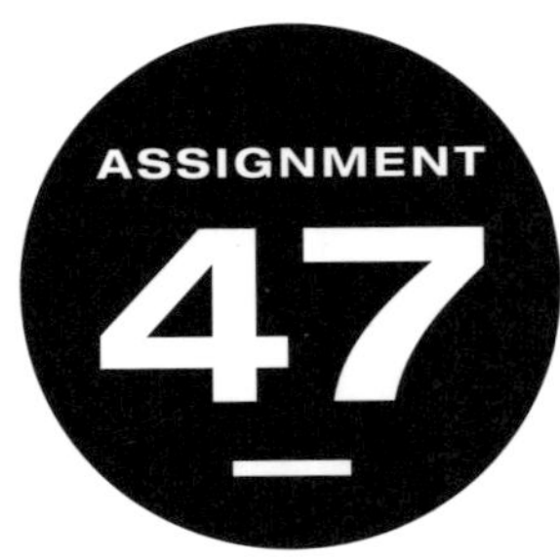

TECHNIQUE

How: Look for current popular tags listed online.

Filters: While there are no particular filters, you can keep an eye out for trendy looks among Instagrammers.

TAGS

Always-popular tags include: #instagood #photooftheday #beautiful #happy

Look also for future trends, including these increasingly popular tags: #life (the essence of "the good life"); #fitness (rising with the inexorable increase in personal health monitoring); #ootd (outfit of the day, which is pushing the still-very-popular #fashion down the list).

PLAY TAG

If you want to promote yourself and your work, you're going to need to get good at playing tag. Naming subjects on your portraits who have their own Instagram accounts is a good way of reaching out, but images in any genre can be assigned hashtags, and it's these tags that can really spread the word and create a global window for your photographs.

There are two contrasting approaches to hashtagging: looking to the past and to the future. The past is the place to find the perennials—the ever-popular tags that keep growing and growing. You're limited to 30 hashtags for any one photo, and choosing a few of these big-hitters is a great start. For this assignment, though, you need to look into the future. Your mission is to identify emerging trends in hashtags, by monitoring and following on-message accounts. Blogs on social media agency sites such as Buffer are also a good source of intelligence. Research the trends, hashtag accordingly, and you will keep your Instagram ahead of the curve.

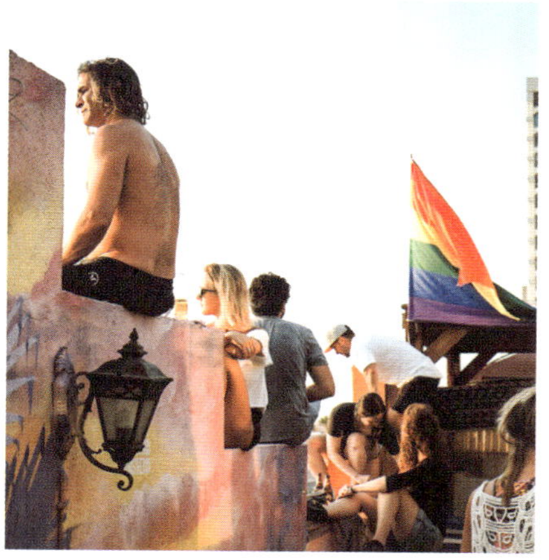

▲ #love

This popular tag has over 1.2 billion Likes on Instagram, so you'll need to go the extra mile to stand out from a very big crowd.

Toa Heftiba
@heftiba.co.uk

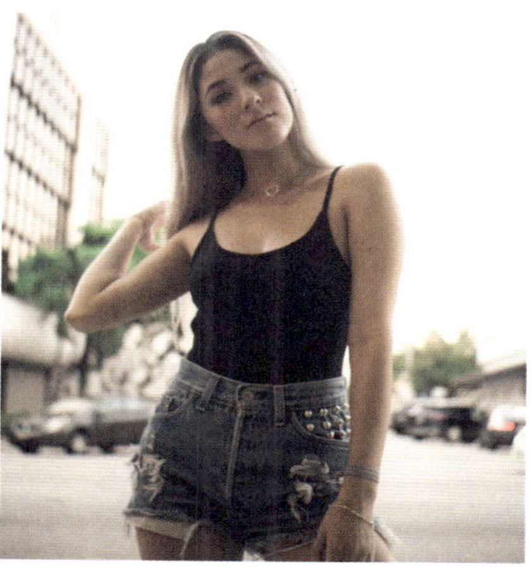

▲ #instagood

Instagood is a tag meaning this is your best photo, or a selfie in which you're looking at your best.

Andre Tan
@andredantan

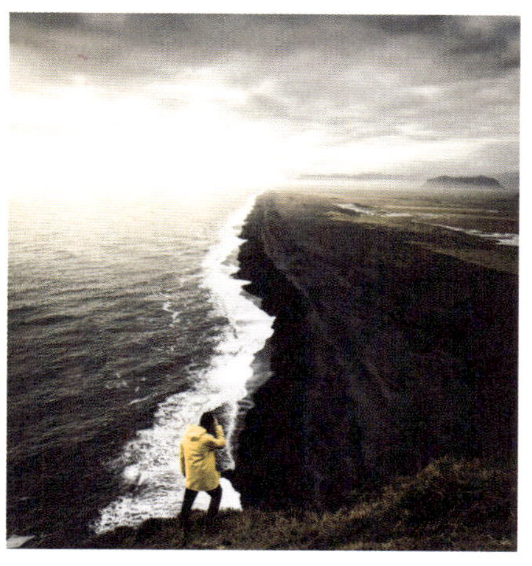

▲ #stayandwander

Stayandwander is a trending travel tag in spite of (or maybe because of) being made up of antonyms (opposites).

Luke Stackpoole
@withluke

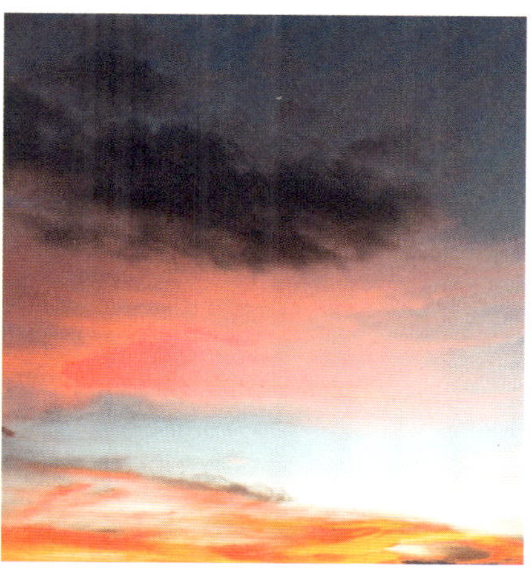

▲ #agameoftones

"Game of tones" is a pun playing on the popularity of the fantasy book and television series, in this case referring to color tones.

Diego PH
@j.diegoph

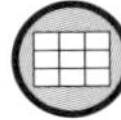
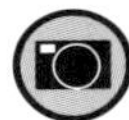
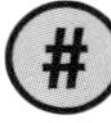

TECHNIQUE

When: The light needs to be good. Early morning offers a golden hour for establishing shots, but overcast/diffuse midday light is good for showing clothing at its best. Also bear in mind times when beauty spots are likely to have fewer tourists.

Where: On vacation, at local beauty spots, or even in front of derelict buildings, but match the location to the fashion.

How: Take a friend as well as your clothes and accessories. Arrange somewhere for you or your model to change if necessary. Pay special attention to lighting, details, and keeping images simple. Remember that you're showing off the clothes, not you!

TAGS

#fashion #contemporaryvulgar
#(featured fashion brands)

#FASHION

Fashion blogging is very big business, and it is really not a surprise that it is a highly competitive subject on Instagram. To have an impact, you need to learn from the best, and produce high-quality images that cut through the noise. Look for a niche. Is there a particular fashion item—hat, necklace, watch, or shoes—that you especially care about? Make it your main focus, and get creative with it.

To achieve the best fashion photography, you will need help both in setting up your shots and taking them, so find a knowledgeable partner. Search for interesting locations, think about how fashion colors work with different backgrounds, and set out to tell a story by imagining a narrative behind your model and their location. Show off the outfits and accessories, always making sure they're the focus of your shots. Light interesting materials carefully, and set busy patterns against plain backgrounds. Your assignment is to create a fashion-conscious set of nine photographs on your Feed that has a unifying style, theme, accessory, material, color, or pattern.

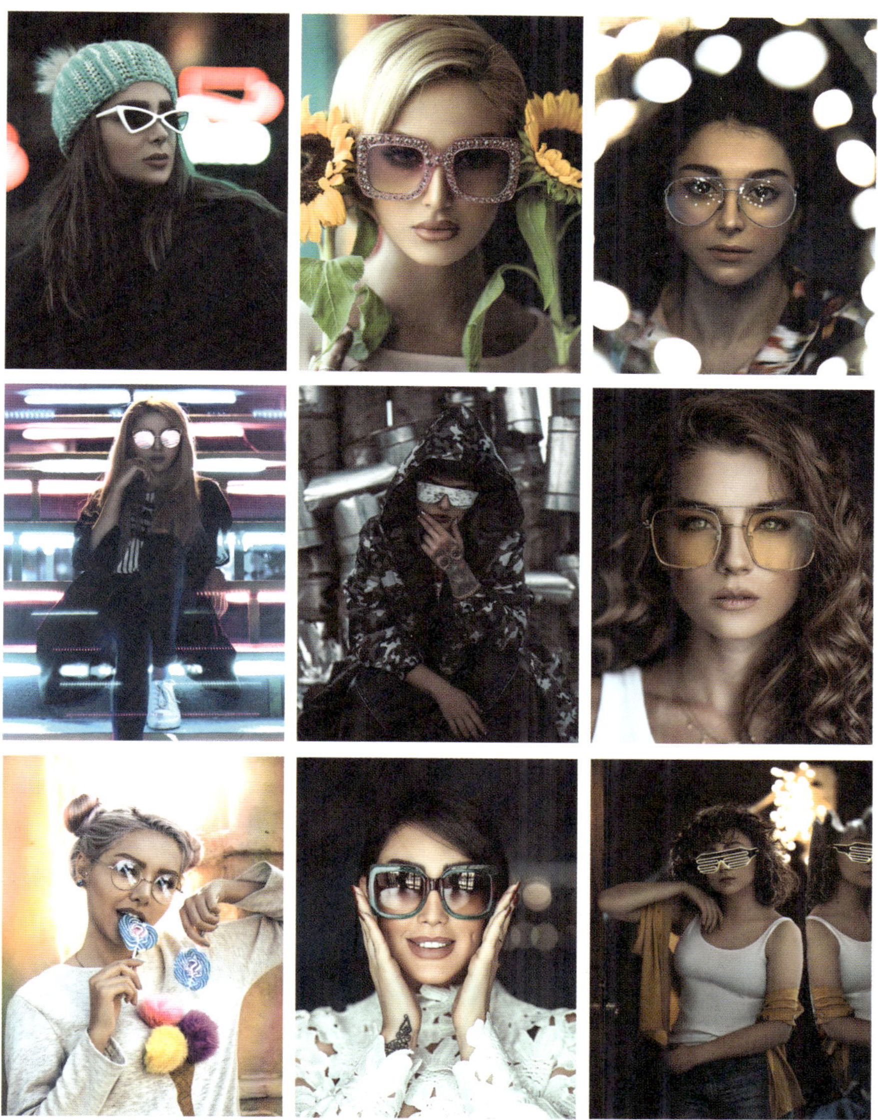

▲ *Ali Pazani is a fashion photographer based in Latvia with a style described as "contemporary vulgar." Note how these fashion shots instantly form a cohesive collection through the consistent use of eye-catching eyeglasses.*

Ali Pazani
@a.pzn

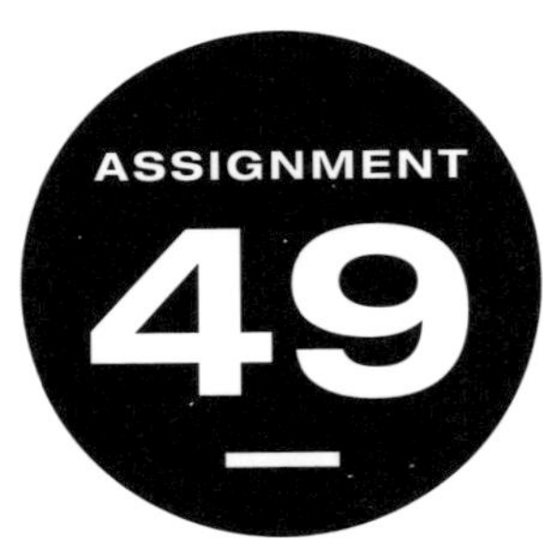

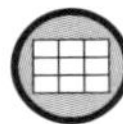

TECHNIQUE

When: Whenever you exercise, eat, or fit into that great new outfit.

Where: In the gym (being careful not to include others in shot, as they may not welcome it), at breakfast, on vacation.

How: Learn to shoot selfies at key moments in your fitness programme, use images to convey your passion, and take care to caption your posts with helpful tips and guides—people are always looking for fitness inspiration and practical advice.

TAGS

#fitness #passion #cycling #rulesofcycling #health #healthylifestyle

A HEALTHY INTEREST

Is staying in shape your thing? Are you a yoga guru, a cycling superhero, or a health food fanatic? A strong subject or personal passion, such as health and fitness, can form the ideal focus for your Instagram photography because you can explore it through images, show it off, and identify a clear group of potential Followers who share an interest. For example, there are over 180 million users of the #fitness hashtag on Instagram, which is a huge potential market for your work.

Your assignment is to take a health or fitness theme and use photography to showcase it on your Feed. If it's fitness, post selfies from your exercise program and provide informative captions about the exercises. If it's healthy eating, share beautiful images of your food (see Assignment 15) and caption with ingredients, recipes, and nutritional information. Always remember the importance of strong captions. People are drawn to practical advice on the Internet, and whether you are offering exercise routines or recipes, hardworking captions and hashtags will encourage more people to share both your passion and your photography.

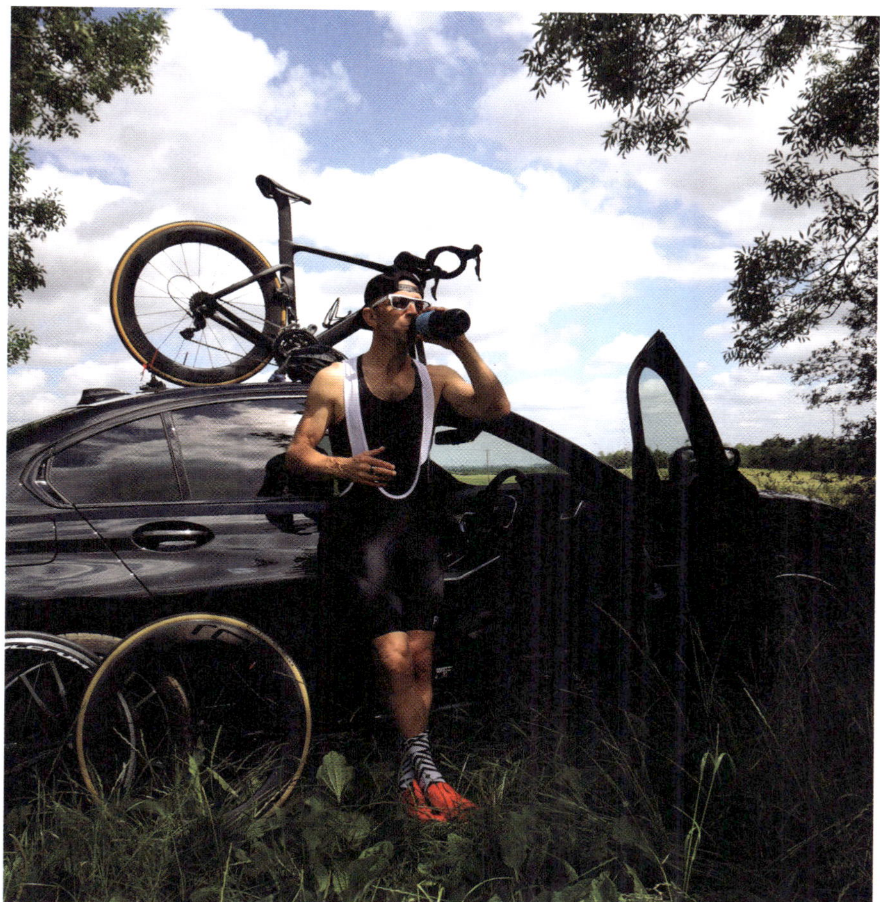

▲ *Jason Bradbury is known for gadgets and bikes, so an image of him kitted out with the latest cycling gear fits his Feed perfectly. A saturated and contrasty filter strengthens the image, while the missing bike wheel draws in the viewer by begging a question that can only be answered by the caption.*

Jason Bradbury
@jasonbradbury

TIP

If your hobby takes you to places where there's nobody available to hold the camera, but you need to hold the lens sufficiently far away to include something as large as a bike or a car, then carry a small tripod for your phone and use the self-timer in the app.

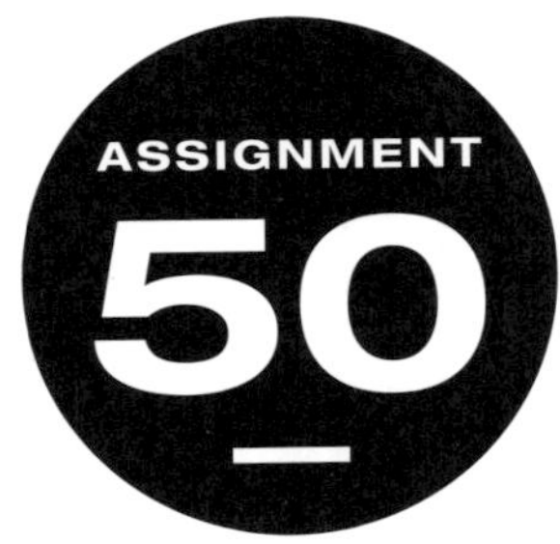

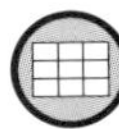

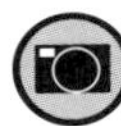

TECHNIQUE

When: When you're engaged in your favorite activity or creating something you want to share.

Where: Shoot anywhere, but it's easier to edit your video when you have access to a computer.

How: Shoot and edit a video on your smartphone to post on IGTV, and use the opportunity to provide something useful to your Followers, such as an instructional video or practical demonstration.

TAGS

After you've created your IGTV video, adding hashtags will increase the chance of the video appearing on people's "For You" pages.

LIGHTS, CAMERA, ACTION

Since 2018, Instagram has been not just a photography and social platform, but also a streaming video platform. There are more than two billion eyeballs out there, and the reigning champion in the video world, YouTube, is more big-screen focused than pocket friendly. For this assignment, your brief is to create a long-form video that is designed specifically for Instagram TV (IGTV).

Shooting a video for the small, vertical screen is probably best done with your smartphone, since it is well adapted to the purpose. If you want to use professional lenses and you have the gear, it's better to shoot in 4K resolution horizontally, if you can, because you'll be cropping a lot of the picture to use it in the vertical format, but you'll also have created footage that you can use in other platforms. You are aiming to create something that will be useful for your audience. For example, if you're a photographer, this could be a video lesson explaining how you composed and processed a particular shot. If your interest is in food or food photography, it could be a cooking demonstration for a particular recipe. This kind of content can have a "long tail," meaning it is popular over a longer period and can help people to find you and your work.

CLICK-BAIT

Put a bit of time into creating a striking
front-page image as you'll be asked for
this when you upload. You can choose
a frame from the video.

EDITING ON YOUR PHONE

Video editing is easier on a computer
because they're more powerful than a
phone and there's a lot more space
to see the "ribbon" or timeline.

ROYALTIES & COPYRIGHT

The easiest way to add a soundtrack is
to use royalty-free music, which you can
buy at a site like pond5.com. Also visit the
YouTube channel Nocopyrightsounds.

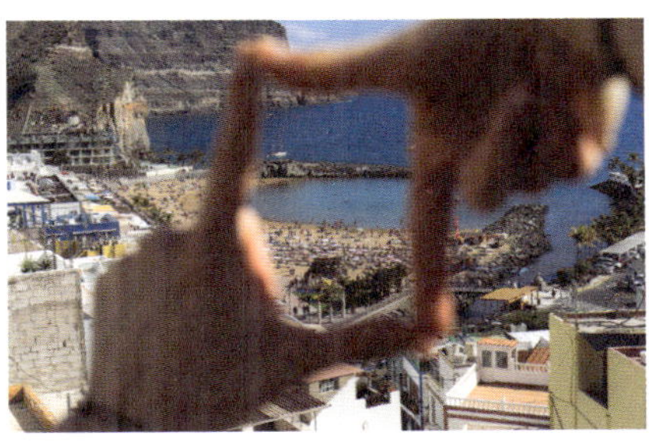

*▲ ▶ Capturing the world is Daniel Gold's
mission, but doing so as stills and for IGTV
isn't always the same thing. You need to
"think vertically" and, if needs be, pan the
camera to reveal the whole scene.*
Dan Gold
@danielcgold

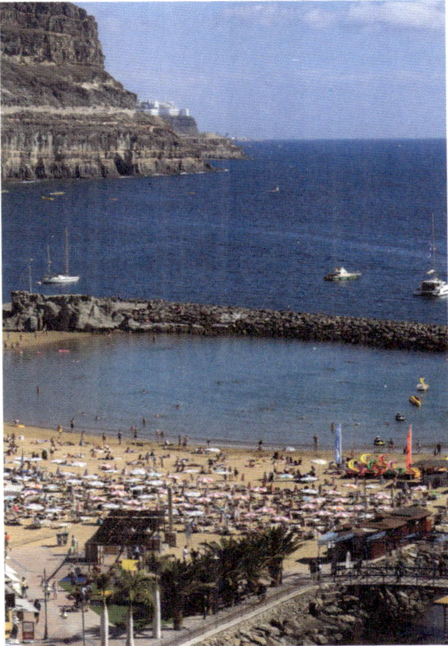

TIPS

- Don't just lock your smartphone or camera on yourself when you're talking—selfie-video
  is hard to watch for more than a few seconds.

- Edit so that there are no long pauses, otherwise viewers will swipe away.

- Make sure the sound is not too loud or too quiet.

- When you write a description for your video, you should give it about 20 words of
  description, then add a "Learn more at…" link (to your own website, for instance).

TECHNIQUE

When: When you want to separate your personal account from your business account, or even a personal account from a public one, so you can adopt different privacy settings for each.

Where: Easier to set up when you have access to a computer.

How: Go to Add Account in the Settings menu, and then Sign Up with Email. Follow the instructions from there.

Filters: Consider using consistent filters throughout all your posts on your second account.

TAGS

As you build your new account, keep a good number of tags on each post—at least 10 up to a maximum of 30.

DOUBLE UP

If you feel you're suffering a split personality on Instagram, and you are looking to build different brands with different identities, then you'll need to create additional accounts. This assignment is a great first step in learning to do that.

Before you begin, ask yourself whether or not you'll be able to keep up with more than one account. You'll also need a different email address for each account, so set those up next. Once you're ready to take the plunge, go to the Settings menu in Instagram—in the top-right options. At the bottom you'll find Add Account, which will take you to a log-in screen. Don't log in, but choose Sign Up from the bottom, then choose Sign Up with Email—you can only use one phone and one Facebook account per Instagram account, so they're likely to already be unavailable. Once you've added your new account, you'll be able to switch between accounts using the icon at the bottom-left corner. When posting, you'll be presented with a list of your connected accounts, but don't be tempted to put the same picture in multiple accounts too often, as that would defeat the object of the exercise. Remember everything you've learned about using photographic styles to develop each account's distinct brand.

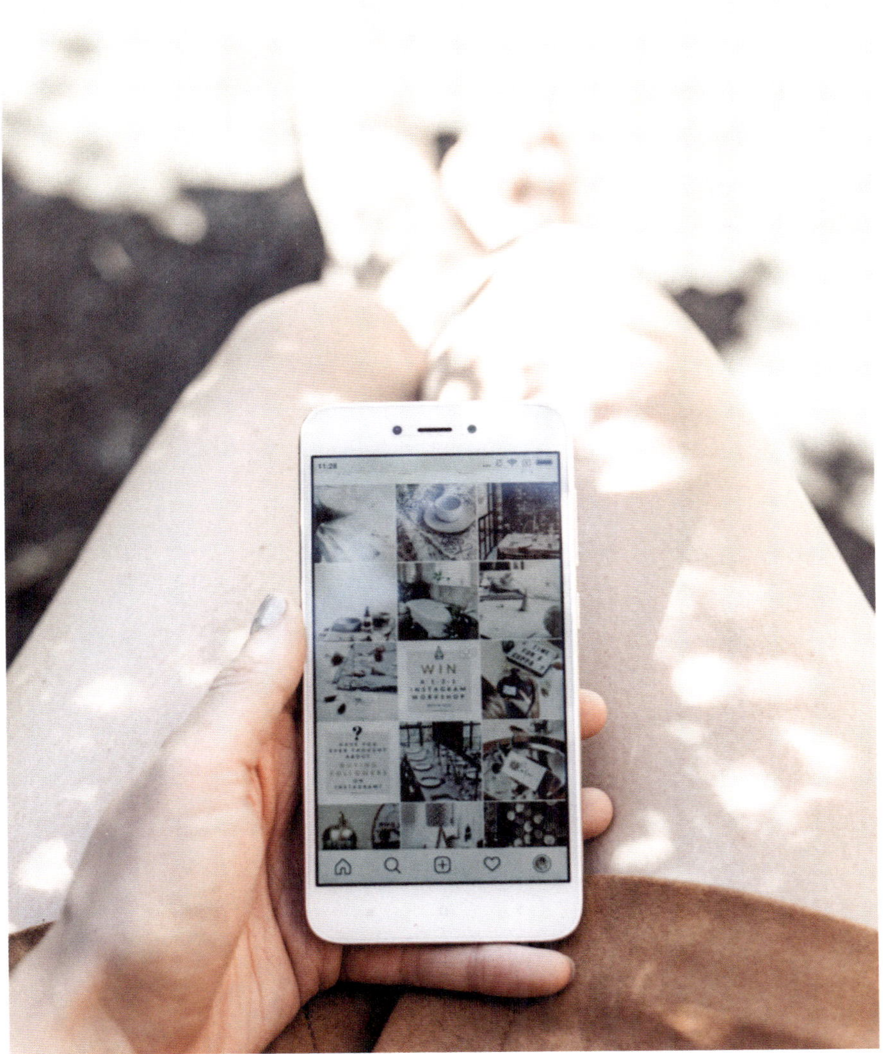

▲ *When you start to build a brand account, you can find copyright-free images online to avoid that empty "new account" look, and mix your product with a positive lifestyle look without incurring much expense.*

Georgia de Lotz
@georgiadelotz

TIP

If you choose to set up an Instagram business account, you'll have access to more analytical tools that will help you to understand and grow your customer base.

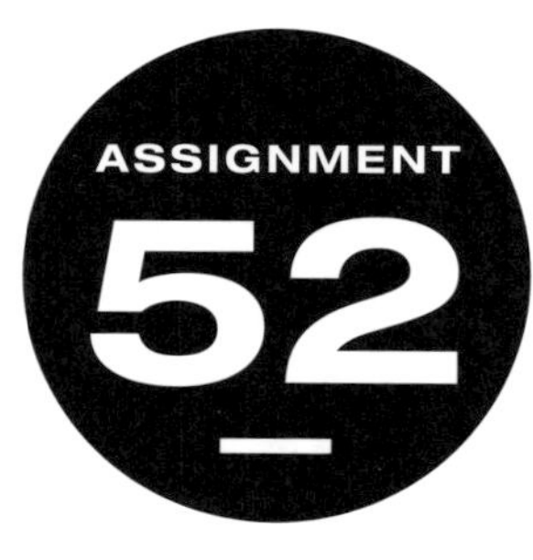

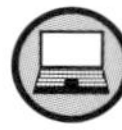

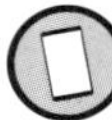

TECHNIQUE

When: When you want to share some old—or new—film prints.

Where: You can photograph prints with a smartphone, so this assignment can be done anywhere.

How: Download a film scanner app and photograph and post your Polaroid or film prints.

Filters: As film prints provide their own special looks that are often imitated by Instagram filters, applying one won't be necessary.

TAGS

#film #filmisnotdead #filmisalive #instantfilm #polaroid

#FILMISNOTDEAD

Instagram isn't just about smartphone cameras. If you love photography, the chances are you'll have experimented with one of the many revival formats, such as Polaroid. You might, too, have a collection of ageing prints lying around. This assignment is about giving old-fashioned film a new lease of life, and sharing your prints on Instagram.

Now that smartphone cameras have reached sufficient quality, it's possible to archive print images simply by taking a photo of them—rather than feeding them slowly into a scanner connected to a computer, and a very handy group of apps have sprung up to help with this. These give you all the fun of shooting real film from the numerous new instant cameras out there, without losing the advantages of digital, not least sharing on social media. Better still, because the manufacturers know quite a lot about their film and how it responds to color, the systems can offer ideal image-correction filters. If you're worried about the shiny, reflective nature of instant photo paper, don't worry—the app developers have thought of that too. The apps will recognize the rectangle and correct it, even if you shoot from the side to eliminate glare, so the result is correctly proportioned. Follow @polaroidoriginals for some idea of what's possible.

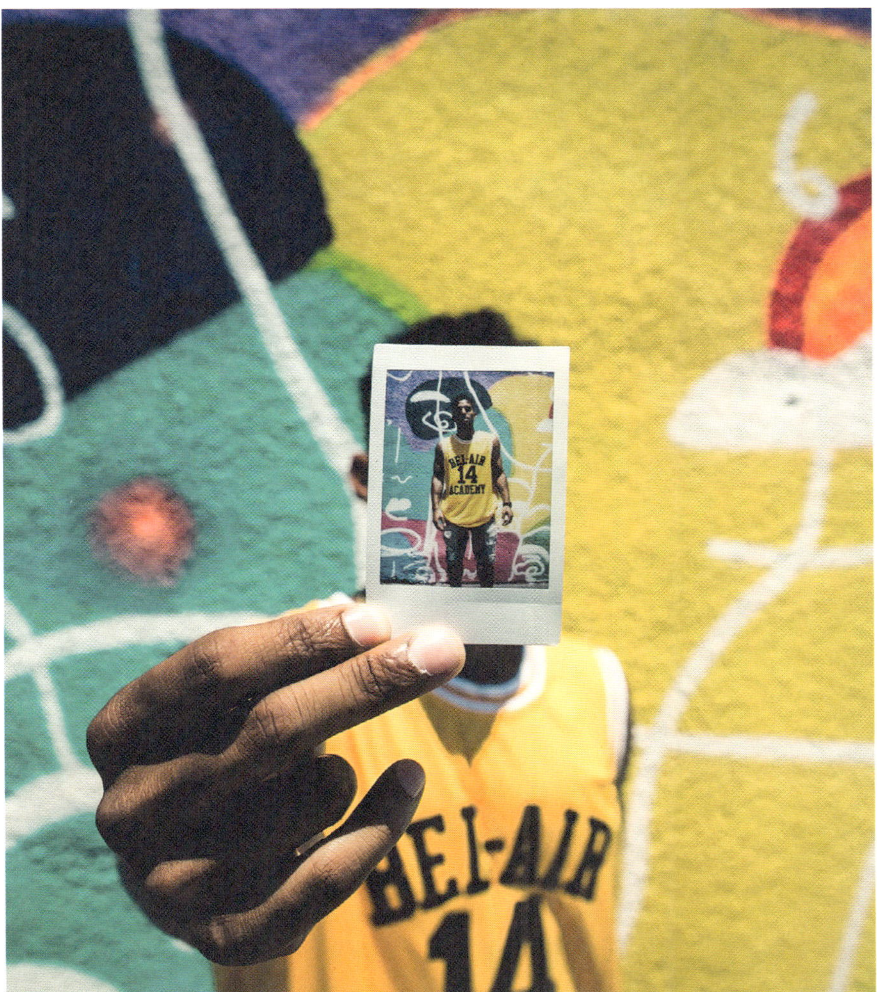

▲ *Film and instant photos of all kinds are rising again; you can show your old school photographic skills with a cheap camera and some film.*

Jakob Owens
@jakobowens

INDEX